New Americans by Choice

New Americans by Choice

Political Perspectives of Latino Immigrants

Harry Pachon
and Louis DeSipio

WITH A FOREWORD BY
Rodolfo O. de la Garza

Routledge
Taylor & Francis Group
LONDON AND NEW YORK

First published 1994 by Westview Press, Inc.

Published 2018 by Routledge
52 Vanderbilt Avenue, New York, NY 10017
2 Park Square, Milton Park, Abingdon, Oxon OX14 4RN

Routledge is an imprint of the Taylor & Francis Group, an informa business

A CIP catalog record for this book is available from the Library of Congress.

ISBN 13: 978-0-367-01197-0 (hbk)
ISBN 13: 978-0-367-16184-2 (pbk)

*To Congressman Edward R. Roybal (Ret.),
who realized early on that U.S. citizenship
is the key to Latino empowerment*

Contents

naturalization process, to having initiated but not completed it, to becoming a citizen. This pattern characterizes all types of civic behavior—from being a church member, to being a member of a social club, to joining the PTA. Also, citizen respondents are more likely to have voted in the United States than in their country of origin, where their major political act appears to have been participating in public marches.

New Americans by Choice is also a unique and excellent source for information directly relevant to the current immigration debate. One of the key questions in that discussion concerns the role immigrants play in the economy. The results clearly indicate that they come for economic reasons. Not only do they have high labor force participation, but they express high job satisfaction even though they have low-status jobs with commensurate incomes. Thus, there is nothing in their profile to suggest they come seeking welfare; moreover, from an employer's perspective, they appear to be "ideal" workers.

On the negative side, the majority have less than a high school education, and many have eight or fewer years of schooling. Given that it is increasingly unlikely that uneducated workers will enjoy much job mobility, these immigrants are likely to remain poor despite their best efforts. They may at some point in their lives, therefore, need to receive government-funded social services. Their work history suggests they will have earned the right to do so through years of active employment and tax paying.

A second issue is whether these immigrants will participate in mainstream American society or remain apart from it. Two measures that help answer this are how immigrants view U.S. society and their language behavior. On both counts, *New Americans by Choice* strongly indicates these immigrants are engaging the mainstream. Not only does the great majority think life is better in the United States than where they came from, but virtually all plan to stay in the United States. Moreover, over 76 percent of Mexicans and more than 90 percent of all others have never returned to visit their home country or have done so one or fewer times per year since they came to the United States. This holds true even though 90 percent have close relations in the homeland.

Although they remain Spanish-dominant, a pattern that is to be expected given that most came as adults, the respondents also manifest substantial English acquisition. Approximately two-thirds consider English to be important or very important to their jobs, a comparable proportion has studied English since they immigrated, and 40 percent indicate they speak English well or very well. This pattern of rapid English acquisition is consistent with findings from other research that suggests "Hispanic immigrants become proficient in English at a more rapid pace than immigrants from other non-English-language countries" (Stevens 1994).

The volume also documents the extent to which there are differences among the several national origin groups. In some instances these are so great that generalizing about Hispanic immigrants is meaningless. For example, 55 percent of Mexicans have 0-8 years of school, while 55 percent of South Americans have at least a high school education. Two percent of Dominicans, compared to approximately 22 percent of Cubans and Central and South Americans have household incomes of $30,000 or more. Almost two-thirds of Cubans are homeowners, compared to 16 percent of Dominicans. Over half of Central and South Americans speak English well or very well, compared to 21 percent of Dominicans.

The groups often are surprisingly varied in their views of the United States. As noted previously, South Americans are more likely than Mexicans to perceive discrimination, but Central Americans are the most likely to do so. Equally noteworthy is that only 11 percent of Dominicans, who tend to be phenotypically dark, report having experienced discrimination compared to 28 percent of South Americans, who are much more light-skinned in appearance.

The groups came with distinct political backgrounds. Overall, few adult immigrants had voted in their homeland, but between one-third and 70 percent of the several national origin groups had participated in marches. Overall, Cubans were among the most politically engaged at home, and Dominicans were twice as likely as Mexicans to have followed politics, voted, or participated in marches in the homeland.

Cubans are the most politically active in the United States. It is particularly noteworthy that over half of the Cuban respondents report contributing money or attending fundraisers in the United States, compared to 15 percent of Mexicans.

Although Mexicans were the least politically active prior to immigrating, they are not the least active once in the United States. To the contrary, even though they register to vote at lower rates than the other groups, Mexican naturalized citizens who are registered voters report higher rates of voting in state and local elections than any of the other groups and are second only to Central Americans with regard to voting in school board elections. It would seem, thus, that whatever attitudes about electoral participation that Mexicans brought with them are quite susceptible to change.

The study also makes us revisit two complicated questions. First, should we as a nation do more to encourage naturalization? The data presented here suggest an emphatic yes. There are many Latino immigrants who want to naturalize but have not done so for a variety of reasons. Those reasons, which are well identified in this study, should be addressed. This means that the application process should be improved to eliminate unnecessary hurdles and to increase the availability of heavily over-subscribed English and citizenship courses. Also, the Immigration and Naturalization Service should do more to emphasize naturalization, as it has begun doing under the newly appointed Commissioner, Doris Meissner. Latino organizations must work with the INS to insure it does its job and to educate immigrants regarding naturalization. Historically, most of these organizations were indifferent to this issue; now, they have followed the lead of the National Association of Latino Elected and Appointed Officials (NALEO) and are ardent naturalization promoters.

It should be noted that not all immigrants are interested in or should be encouraged to naturalize. One perspective on naturalization is that it is a rational decision about maximizing benefits (Jasso 1994). While a factor in any judgment, such calculations are not central to the decision for most Latino immigrants (Alvarez 1987). Naturalization is an act that fundamentally affects one's identity and, thus, it is emotionally and psychologically expensive. Approximately 15 percent of Latino immigrants eligible for naturalization are not ready to make this transition (DeSipio 1993). Neither the state nor ethnic interest groups should encourage naturalization among those who are not interested in making this change.

This leads to the second question: why should immigrants naturalize? The volume is less clear on this. Even though the overwhelming majority of respondents are favorably disposed to doing so, relatively few do. In part, as the study points out, this is because the process is unnecessarily complicated and costly. Given that the majority of Mexicans, almost half of Dominicans, and over a third of Central and South Americans have never even begun the process, it seems that there is more to it than that, however.

One important factor may be that it is possible to be an active and virtually full member of American society without being a citizen. The most obvious benefits unavailable to these non-citizens are the right to vote and to hold certain types of jobs. Because few are likely to meet the educational requirements of those jobs that require citizenship, in reality the only real loss is the right to vote. However, given that most of these immigrants have no history of voting prior to immigrating, it is unlikely that the inability to vote here is perceived to be a major loss. Thus, it is not surprising that of those who have not initiated or completed the naturalization process, almost one-third indicate they see no benefits to becoming a citizen as a very important reason for not naturalizing, and only 52 and 69 percent think it is very important to become a citizen. This even though 80 percent agree that life is better here than in the homeland, and almost 100 percent plan to live here permanently.

New Americans by Choice, in sum, does not completely answer why more Latino immigrants do not naturalize. It does, however, indicate that most of these immigrants are significantly affected by their experiences in the United States. Even though they are poorly paid in low-status jobs, they think life is better here than in their homeland. They learn English, they become more attentive to and involved with politics, and their participation in civil society increases as they go through the naturalization process. *New Americans by Choice*, then, tells us that even though Mexicans may differ from South Americans on some of these dimensions, and from Dominicans on others, overall these immigrants appear to behave the way immigrants did before them. Whether or not they naturalize, they contribute to and support the society and polity.

There is, in other words, nothing about any of these groups that threatens the social or political fabric of our society. Why, then, have so many Americans been so unwelcoming of these newcomers? If we as a nation were more open and generous in our attitudes, perhaps more immigrants would take the next step and formally join the polity. That is another question that this volume makes us ask but does not answer.

New Americans by Choice is certain to become a basic reference for anyone interested in Latino immigrants and the impact they are likely to have on the future of Latino politics in the United States. Given that Latinos can only become politically and demographically more important as we move into the next century, this volume will also be of value to anyone interested in the future of our nation.

Rodolfo O. de la Garza
Austin, TX

References

Alvarez, Robert. 1987. "A Profile of the Citizenship Process Among Hispanics in the United States." *International Migration Review* 21 (2) (Summer): 327-351.

Center for Immigration Studies. 1994. *Backgrounder* 1 (94) (May): 9.

de la Garza, Rodolfo O.; Louis DeSipio; F. Chris Garcia; John A. Garcia; and Angelo Falcon. 1992. *Latino Voices: Mexican, Puerto Rican, and Cuban Perspectives on American Politics*. Boulder, CO: Westview Press.

DeSipio, Louis. 1993. "Counting on the Latino Vote: Latinos as a New Electorate." Ph.D. Dissertation, University of Texas at Austin.

Fuchs, Lawrence H. 1990. *The American Kaleidoscope: Race, Ethnicity and the Civic Culture*. Hanover, N.H.: The University Press of New England.

Garcia, F. Chris; Rodolfo O. de la Garza; John A. Garcia; and Angelo Falcon. 1994. "Still Looking for Constructive Critique." Response to *Still Looking for America: Beyond the Latino National Political Survey*. Typescript. Albuquerque, N.M. February 18.

Jasso, Guillermina. 1994. "Presentation to the NALEO Citizenship Conference." In NALEO Educational Fund. *Proceedings of the National Citizenship Conference*, pp. 114-120. Washington, D.C.: NALEO Educational Fund.

Schlesinger, Jr., Arthur M. 1991. *The Disuniting of America: Reflections on a Multicultural Society*. New York: W. W. Norton and Company.

Stanford Center for Chicano Research. 1994. *Still Looking for America: Beyond the*

Latino National Political Survey. Stanford Center for Chicano Research: Public Outreach Project, Stanford University. January.

Stevens, Gillian. 1994. "Immigration, Emigration, Language Acquisition, and the English Language Proficiency of Immigrants in the United States." In Barry Edmonston and Jeffrey S. Passel, eds. *Immigration and Ethnicity*. Washington, D.C.: The Urban Institute.

1

Immigrants and Naturalized Citizens: Developing the National Latino Immigrant Survey

Once I sought to write a history of immigrants in America. Then I discovered that the immigrants were *American history.*

—Oscar Handlin
The Uprooted

From the point of view of citizenship, there are two kinds of Americans—those who are American involuntarily by birth and those who are American by choice.

—John Palmer Gavitt
Americans by Choice

As a nation, the United States proudly acknowledges its immigrant roots. Virtually all Americans can trace their ancestries to immigrant forbearers. With the benefit of hindsight, we can now see that the descendants of previous generations of immigrants have found or made a welcoming environment (Fuchs 1990). While this welcoming environment may not have existed when many first generation immigrants arrived, the U.S. Constitution assured that their children and all native-born individuals would have a formal legal equality based on citizenship.

Painful exceptions to the general pattern of immigrant incorporation darken American history. Africans forced into migration to the United States did not receive formal equal rights for the first three hundred and fifty years of residence. Asians faced statutory barriers to immigration and naturalization of a kind not imposed on any other group of immigrants to these shores; indeed, during World War II, they saw their rights as citizens explicitly denied. Mexicans, both those living in the Southwest prior to its annexation by the United States and those who migrated in the century afterward, faced formal and informal barriers that precluded most from attaining equal citizenship.

With each new wave of immigrants, the nation has been tested to assure that immigrants and their children come to be the formal equals of the native-born. In the cases of Africans, Asians, and Mexicans, the nation repeatedly failed this test until very recently. Similarly, many first generation immigrants from other parts of the world faced a hostile and unwelcoming environment. Despite these clear and uncontestable failures of incorporation, the long-term impact of continuing waves of immigration has been to repeatedly challenge the political system to live up to ideals of equal opportunity and equality before the law, regardless of race, ethnicity, or national origin (DeSipio and de la Garza 1992).

While the political system has met this challenge in the past for most immigrants, it has done so after an initial reluctance. Throughout U.S. history, the dominant society has viewed the newest immigrants as less likely to Americanize than previous immigrants. This was said as far back as the 1790s; it was said again in the 1840s, the 1910s, and is being said again today. This recurring perception—that new immigrants vaguely threaten the nation—forces the nation to incorporate the new immigrants that it has decided to admit to its shores.

Over time, the opportunity for admission has narrowed. Prior to the 1920s, the borders were largely uncontrolled and the nation had to incorporate whomever arrived. In 1920, the foreign-born constituted 13.2 percent of the national population. Today, at least in terms of immigration to a status that permits naturalization, the borders are controlled and the nation can decide whom it will eventually incorporate. Despite immigration that is unprecedented in terms of raw volume, the foreign-born constituted just 7.9 percent of the national population in 1990 (U.S. Bureau of the Census 1993*d*: Table 54).

Nevertheless, the nation again faces the need to incorporate a large number of immigrants. The latest wave of immigrants was prompted by changes in the immigration law in 1965. As had happened with previous waves of immigrants, this newest group differs from its predecessors. Today, immigrants are much more likely to come from Asia, Latin America, or Africa than were pre-1965 immigrants. Again, in a pattern reminiscent of earlier periods of heightened immigration, the political incorporation of the immigrant has lagged behind the immigration. Thus in contemporary public policy debates, political inclusion of the immigrant has been relegated to a topic of secondary importance (Pachon 1991; DeSipio and de la Garza 1992). From the 1960s to the 1980s, when policymakers mentioned immigration issues, they were concerned with undocumented immigration, refugees, or ceilings on the numbers of immigrants this country should receive. They focused little attention on the political integration of the immigrant into American society.

A vast sea change on the topic of immigration has occurred in the

1990s. At the national level, immigration policy is gaining new levels of saliency (Mydans 1993; Pierce 1993). Policymakers continue to discuss the control of undocumented immigration, the reduction of annual immigrant ceilings, and the reconsideration of refugee policy. These traditional issues, however, are not the only immigration-related issues being discussed (Barnes 1993; Schneider 1993). State and local leaders have placed anti-immigrant sentiments into the immigration policy debate (Hamilton 1993; Rohter 1994; Freedman 1994). These leaders, including members of Congress, the governor of California, and candidates for national and local elective office throughout the country, are proposing draconian policy solutions to stop undocumented immigration, policies that would have been politically untenable in earlier decades (Decker 1992; "Immigration Control: Doing It Right" 1993; Kiely 1993; Pressley 1993; Simon and Ramsey 1994). These draconian reactions are being considered in major national forums.

Equally significantly, however, discussion about immigration policy is now expanding to include immigrant policy (Bach 1991; de la Garza and DeSipio 1993). Policymakers are beginning to explore the role that government should play in the lives of immigrants once they are settled in this country (Garza 1993). The government's role in promoting naturalization has become a particular focus of attention. The Commissioner of the Immigration and Naturalization Service (INS), for example, has proposed reversing a long-standing agency policy of not promoting naturalization among eligible immigrants (Duarte 1985; Pear 1993).

The emergence of naturalization as a topic of national policy sets the context for this work. The National Latino Immigrant Survey (NLIS) is the first survey of legal Latino[1] immigrants in this nation. The study, undertaken before naturalization received national media attention, looks at an increasingly significant segment of our nation's immigrant population—the legal immigrant from Latin America who has naturalized or who has sufficient residence to be eligible for U.S. citizenship.

Latino Immigration to the United States

Only a small portion of the country's Latino population can trace its ancestry to the United States's purchase of Florida in 1819 or to the annexation of Texas and the territory encompassing the states of Arizona, California, Colorado, and New Mexico in 1848. Indeed, most Latinos are recent immigrants (Passel and Edmonston 1991). In 1992, 35 percent of all Latinos and more than 40 percent of Latino adults were foreign-born (U.S. Bureau of the Census 1991*a*; 1993*a*; 1993*b*). In California, Illinois, and Florida, close to half of Latino adults are first generation immigrants who have not naturalized and are thus not eligible to vote (U.S. Bureau of the Census 1993c).

Many observers do not understand these variations in Latino citizenship and residency status. To most, including many policymakers, Latinos fall under two simple categories—Latino immigrants, who many Americans perceive as being illegal aliens, and all other Latinos, the native-born. The reality of the legal status of Latinos in this country is considerably more complex. Significant segments of the adult Latino population include:

- native-born citizens;
- foreign-born Latinos who have become U.S. citizens through naturalization;
- foreign-born Latinos who have not resided in the United States long enough (usually five years) to be eligible to naturalize;
- foreign-born Latinos with sufficient residence who have not naturalized;
- foreign-born formerly undocumented Latino immigrants who qualified for legal permanent resident status under the Immigration Reform Control Act of 1986 and began to achieve eligibility for naturalization in 1993;
- agricultural workers who received legal permanent resident status under the Immigration Reform Control Act of 1986 who will begin to be eligible to naturalize in 1994;
- foreign-born Latino immigrants awarded temporary resident status in the United States as refugees or asylees;
- tourists and other short-term visitors to the United States; and
- foreign-born Latino undocumented immigrants who do not fall into the above categories.

While society has focused considerable attention on the growing political potential of U.S. citizen Hispanics as well as on the problems associated with Latino undocumented immigrants, the staggeringly high number of Latino legal immigrants has been consistently overlooked by the media, political analysts, and even at times by the scholarly community (Pachon 1987; DeSipio 1987, 1993). As Table 1.1 illustrates, Latino legal immigration to this country has constituted a significant segment of all legal immigration to the nation for the past six decades. As Table 1.2 shows, the cumulative impact of this immigration—high rates of Latino non-citizenship—is pronounced in those states with large Latino populations.

TABLE 1.1 Legal Latino Immigration to the United States as a Share of Total Immigration, 1940-1992

	Total Immigration	*Percent Latino of Legal Immigrants*
1941-1950	1,035,039	15
1951-1960	2,515,479	22
1961-1970	3,321,677	35
1971-1980	4,493,314	36
1981-1990	7,338,062[1]	42[1]
1991	1,827,167[1]	54[1]
1992	973,977[1]	32[1]

[1]Includes legalization applicants under the Immigration Reform and Control Act of 1986.

Source: Authors' calculations based on U.S. Immigration and Naturalization Service (1993).

TABLE 1.2 Numbers and Percent of Latino Foreign-Born Population by State, 1990.

	Latino Population	*Latino Foreign-Born*	*Foreign-Born as a Share of the State Latino Population %*
Arizona	680,628	160,391	24
California	7,557,550	3,438,516	45
Colorado	419,332	41,314	10
Florida	1,555,031	853,069	55
Illinois	878,682	342,083	39
New Jersey	720,344	251,668	35
New Mexico	576,709	53,411	9
New York	2,151,743	683,014	32
Texas	4,294,120	1,036,831	24

Source: Authors' calculations based on U.S. Bureau of the Census 1993a.

The Impact to the Hispanic Community of High Numbers of Foreign-Born

The large numbers of legal Latino non-citizens who are permanently residing in this country have consequences for American society at large and the Hispanic community. The powerlessness and political alienation that many have attributed to the Hispanic community may result in part from the presence of large numbers of legal residents. These permanent resident aliens raise expectations for political clout, but are excluded from participation in many aspects of the political process (de la Garza and DeSipio 1993; Pachon and Arguelles 1994).

Other civic consequences of non-citizenship limit the political voices of Latinos. For instance, non-citizens cannot hold elective office or serve on juries. The latter is relevant because of the persistent underrepresentation of Hispanics on juries in most urban areas. Thus, this underrepresentation may be attributable not only to institutional discrimination, e.g., exclusion of Hispanics from jury selection panels, but also to the lack of a large pool of eligible Hispanic citizens to serve as jurors.

The lack of citizenship also restricts Hispanics' economic mobility. These restrictions include:

- exclusion from most federal government positions, state and local public safety positions, and in some states, public school teaching positions;
- exclusion from certain positions in the defense industries that require security clearances;
- exclusion from full Social Security benefits if retired and living abroad;
- denial of the right to travel abroad for unrestricted periods of time; and
- the inability to immigrate immediate relatives outside the immigration preference system.

Finally, and most importantly from a political perspective, U.S. citizenship confers the right to vote, and non-citizenship prevents Latino immigrants from participating in the electoral process of this country. Any look at the voting statistics of Latinos highlights the significance of U.S. citizenship. Over 80 percent of the difference in voter turnout between Latinos and African Americans can be explained by non-citizenship among Latinos (Pachon and DeSipio 1992: Table One). In certain states, California and Florida, for example, low rates of U.S. citizenship may be the single largest obstacle to electoral empowerment in the Hispanic community (U.S. Bureau of the Census 1993*c*).

Another overlooked political consequence of non-citizenship is the potential effect on accountability ties between publicly elected officials and their constituents. For example, the 1990 census revealed that 70 congressional districts had more than 100,000 Latino constituents (National Association of Latino Elected Officials [NALEO] 1993). Yet the voting records of representatives from many of these districts do not reflect the concerns articulated by Latino political activists.

Thus, U.S. citizenship is not merely a symbolic status acquired by the immigrant. It confers on the naturalized citizen a set of rights and responsibilities nearly equal to native-born American citizens.[2]

Naturalization and the Latino Community

As early as 1983, the National Association of Latino Elected Officials (NALEO) Educational Fund recognized that U.S. citizenship was a major obstacle to the Hispanic community's political empowerment. Initially, at least, citizenship also appeared to be a difficult barrier for immigrants to overcome. A review of naturalization data reported by the INS reveals that immigrants from most parts of Latin America have some of the lowest naturalization rates of all immigrants. Some notable exceptions are worthy of mention. In the early 1980s, Cuban Americans naturalized soon after becoming eligible. Some nationalities, most notably Canadians, naturalized at the same low rates as Latin American and Caribbean immigrants. Despite these exceptions, however, the evidence indicated that Latinos were slow to naturalize and arguably less interested in becoming U.S. citizens than were immigrants from elsewhere. While these data appeared to show that Latinos were less interested than other immigrants in United States citizenship, they provide little understanding of why Latinos would have a lower propensity to naturalize.

The Conventional Wisdom: Latino Immigrant Disinterest in Naturalization

NALEO's discussions with government officials, Latino community activists, elected officials, and others uncovered a widely held perception that Latino immigrants were not interested in acquiring the rights and benefits of U.S. citizenship. Although the specific explanations varied, many thought the problem was rooted in Latino immigrant culture rather than a failure of the receiving society to integrate the new arrivals. Among the explanations repeatedly offered for this perception were:

> "Mexicans/Latinos don't want to become U.S. citizens because they are loyal to their home countries."
>
> "Latino immigrants are not here permanently. They plan to return home so they choose to retain their nationality."
>
> "Latino immigrants, especially Mexican immigrants, fear mistreatment by the INS so they don't apply for citizenship."
>
> "Mexican immigrants lose their property rights if they become U.S. citizens. They therefore choose to remain Mexican citizens."
>
> "Since many Latino immigrants have low levels of education, the citizenship exam is a formidable hurdle that few wish to undertake."
>
> "Since Latinos experience discrimination, they are reluctant to become citizens of a society that discriminates against them."

Despite the pervasiveness of these views, several indicators suggested that there might be more to the story than immigrants' nationalism for their home countries. The first indicator was historical. At the end of the most recent period of large-scale immigration to the United States (roughly from 1880 to 1920), a scholarly debate raged over the propensity of the then "new" immigrants—Southern and Eastern Europeans—to naturalize (Gavitt 1971 [1922]; Carpenter 1927; Guest 1980). Although there were some slight differences in naturalization propensity between these "new" immigrants and the "old" Northeastern Europeans, the largest single factor explaining the lower naturalization rates of the new group was its length of residence in the United States. A series of studies of the new immigrants' attachment to the United States indicated that they had in fact sought to join the polity with the same intensity as had the old. As we began our study, we wondered if there was a parallel in the 1920s to today's perceptions that the newer immigrants were less likely to Americanize. We were, then, open to the notion that a simple reading of raw naturalization rates might obscure a deeper understanding about Latino attachment to the United States and propensity to naturalize.[3]

The second indicator that raised doubts about the conventional wisdom concerning Latino immigrant disinterest in naturalization emerged from a more detailed analysis of INS data. Unpublished data indicated that many more immigrants, both Latino and non-Latino, sought naturalization than received it. This finding showed that there was interest, but that statutory and bureaucratic impediments blocked interested immigrants from reaching their goal (DeSipio and Pachon 1992).

Furthermore, the conventional wisdom ran the risk of becoming self-fulfilling. To the extent that Latino leaders, policymakers, immigrant advocates, and others believed that Latinos did not want to naturalize, they would make little effort to encourage this. Again, the historical example demonstrated that previous generations of immigrants had had access to extensive assistance with naturalization both from within the ethnic community and from without (Peel 1935; Myers 1968 [1917]; Erie 1988). To the extent that these services were not available to Latino immigrants, the immigrants might well not seek naturalization.

Clearly, none of these concerns individually refuted the conventional wisdom that Latino immigrants were not interested in U.S. citizenship. Yet, they raised sufficient doubts to encourage further investigation into the question of why Latinos were less likely to naturalize.

The NALEO National U.S. Citizenship Project

In 1984, with support from the Gannett and Gulf foundations, NALEO convened a group of academics, policymakers, and community activists to probe why Latino immigrants had such low rates of naturalization (NALEO 1985). It quickly became apparent that while there was much anecdotal evidence on the issue of U.S. citizenship and the Hispanic community, little rigorous research had been done. Despite the absence of empirical research, the participants in the conference believed that non-citizenship would be an issue of increasing importance to the Latino community. It was clear that extensive methodologically sound research needed to be undertaken.

NALEO then approached the Ford Foundation. With the support of Dr. William A. Diaz, foundation program officer, NALEO initiated an ambitious five-year research and demonstration project on the reasons for low rates of U.S. citizenship in the Latino community. The authors of this book served as Principal Investigator and Senior Research Associate.

Initially, the project had three major components: a review of social science research on naturalization and a re-analysis of existing social science databases focusing on naturalization; an administrative analysis of INS naturalization activities; and a field study of community and non-profit organizations engaged in promoting U.S. citizenship. In order to assure that the project benefitted from previous social science research, NALEO formed a social science advisory committee. The members of this committee were: Dr. William A. Diaz, the Ford Foundation; Dr. Leo Estrada, University of California, Los Angeles; Dr. Alejandro Portes, Johns Hopkins University; and Dr. Lou Tornatzky, Industrial Technology Institute.

The NALEO research staff and the social science advisory committee commissioned a re-analysis of the two major data sets that contained data on the interest in and the propensity to naturalize: the Chicano Survey and the Portes/National Science Foundation study of Mexican and Cuban Immigrants (Garcia 1987; Portes and Curtis 1987). While these surveys offered valuable insights, we soon realized that existing social science databases did not offer sufficient data on Latinos and naturalization to test our hypotheses about the causes of low rates of Latino naturalization. Instead, the dearth of research on this topic necessitated that we commission a national survey of Latino permanent resident immigrants and naturalized citizens. This survey, the results of which are presented in this volume, needed to generate three types of data. First, it needed to develop a demographic portrait of Latino permanent resident immigrants. Second, it needed to examine Latino immigrant political attitudes and behaviors, both in the country of origin and in the United States. Finally, it needed to examine the impact of various naturalization requirements, both statutory and bureaucratic, on Latino immigrants interested in becoming U.S. citizens.

Initially, our thinking about the survey and the types of hypotheses to test was influenced by the conventional wisdoms previously cited. As we proceeded to implement the survey, however, we began to receive information that refuted the contention that most Latinos are not interested in U.S. citizenship. The first contradictory information came from the increase in Latino naturalization that coincided with the onset of NALEO's citizenship promotion campaign in 1985. The number of Mexican naturalizations, for example, increased from approximately 15,000 in 1984 to 28,000 in 1986. In this same two-year period, naturalizations among former citizens of Latin American countries increased from approximately 52,000 to 71,000 (U.S. Immigration and Naturalization Service 1988). Despite their perceived lack of interest in naturalization, Mexican immigrants were regularly one of the top three nationalities to naturalize in the late 1980s and early 1990s (U.S. Immigration and Naturalization Service 1992).

A second source of contradictory information was the Hispanic community's dramatic response to a toll-free citizenship hotline established by NALEO in 1985 to provide naturalization information. Within three days of announcing the hotline in Southern California, six thousand callers attempted to contact the hotline. Similarly, when the hotline was publicized in Texas, NALEO received twenty thousand calls in the first month. In eight years of operation, the NALEO citizenship hotline has received over half a million calls. The increase in naturalizations and the positive response to NALEO's citizenship initiative raised serious challenges to the conventional wisdom that "Latinos don't want to become U.S. citizens."

The National Latino Immigrant Survey explores this question and many others regarding Latino immigrant attitudes towards U.S. citizenship. Methodologically, the NLIS had to overcome several obstacles. The first was whether a survey of this type was feasible since a national survey of the Hispanic immigrant had never been attempted through telephone interviews. Moreover, the survey population was thought to be difficult to reach, because of perceived suspicion of telephone surveys, the dispersion of the immigrant population, and the high incidence of unlisted telephone numbers. Some survey researchers opined that Latino immigrants would not answer "sensitive" questions over the telephone about their immigration experiences or attitudes towards the INS. Indeed, the difficulty of reaching this population was considerable, since foreign-born Hispanic immigrants legally residing in the United States were less than 2 percent of the total 1980 U.S. population (see Appendix Two for full details).

The research staff decided that the NLIS would limit its sample to Hispanics living in the forty-seven counties that accounted for 80 percent of all foreign-born Hispanic adults living in the United States at the time of the 1980 census. In these counties, Latino immigrants with five years of permanent residence constituted one in fifteen of the screened households instead of one in fifty-five nationwide. To reach our final sample of 1,636, we called 74,430 phone numbers. These calls resulted in 4,923 households with Hispanic residents. Among these households with a Latino member, 2,942 had no household members who met the screening criteria. Of the remaining 1,985 qualified households, NALEO interviewed 1,636.

Findings

The National Latino Immigrant Survey is more than a survey of Latino immigrant attitudes towards U.S. citizenship. The survey documents the political, social and cultural, and economic worlds of the Latino immigrant. These general findings about the Latino immigrant serve as a backdrop to the more specific findings on Latino immigrants and naturalization. In light of the survey's findings, many of society's assumptions about Latino immigrants will need to be reexamined.

Foremost among these assumptions is that Latino immigrants are here temporarily and are planning to return to their homelands upon accumulation of savings or upon retirement. In fact, the National Latino Immigrant Survey conclusively documents that Latino immigrants were planning to make the U.S. their permanent home and considered the United States a better place to live than their native country.

A second assumption is that Latino immigrants are isolated in separatist barrios or ghettos. To the contrary, the National Latino Immigrant Survey reveals that while these first-generation immigrants still predominantly socialized and worked with other Latino peers, their commitment to permanent settlement in American society was high and they were acculturating.

A final assumption is that Latino permanent resident immigrants are an economic drain on society. The data presented here could not more clearly refute this notion. Latino permanent resident immigrants, at least those with five or more years of legal residence, were contributing members of the U.S. economy. They manifested high levels of labor force participation and had household incomes that, on average, exceeded those for Latinos as a whole (native and foreign-born), for the same year. While there were wide variations on each of these indicators by national origin, this sketch demonstrates that long-term permanent residents and naturalized U.S. citizens from Latin America and the Caribbean were active contributing members of the U.S. economy.

Latino Immigrants' Attitudes Towards Naturalization

Perhaps the most surprising finding of the National Latino Immigrant Survey was the widespread desire of Latino permanent resident immigrants to naturalize and the intensity of this desire. This interest in U.S. citizenship was much higher than the conventional wisdom at the project's start would have predicted. Fully nine out of ten Latino immigrants believed that becoming a U.S. citizen is very or somewhat important. About one out of three eligible Latino immigrants had naturalized. Even this baseline figure was not available prior to the completion of the NLIS.

Although most Latino immigrants recognized the importance of U.S. citizenship, for many, this belief had not translated into a political attachment to the United States. Nevertheless, more than 40 percent of Latino immigrants did report that they identified more with the United States than with their home country. Only slightly more reported primary political attachment to the country of origin.

When asked to identify the most important reason for seeking U.S. citizenship, respondents largely expressed a desire for access to political participation. Their second most likely category of responses related to access to economic opportunities and specific government benefits; however, these self-interested responses were mentioned by far fewer Latino immigrants.

Why Don't Latinos Become Citizens?

The survey not only indicates the magnitude of the desire for citizenship, but also some of the reasons why many immigrants are unable to attain this objective. Although only one in three Latino immigrants became a U.S. citizen, one out of two initiated the process by obtaining the naturalization forms or by taking English or civics classes to prepare for naturalization. Thus, half of the Latino immigrant population who initiated this process were unable to complete it by the time of the survey. Although it is not possible to provide an exact count of these unsuccessful citizenship-seekers nationwide, it is fair to suggest that there are between 1,000,000 and 1,500,000 in the Latino community alone.[4]

Paradoxically, even though non-U.S. citizens viewed U.S. citizenship as an important goal, approximately one-third did not apply for citizenship because they did not consider it as a possibility.

When asked about a range of reasons for not seeking citizenship, Latino non-citizens ranked the absence of benefits as the most important reason for not naturalizing. Second, they expressed concern that the INS examination would be too difficult. Considering the low educational levels of Latino immigrants, the fear of a civics and English test is not hard to understand. Unexpectedly, the survey indicated that immigrants who *did* take the examination tended to view it as not difficult. The third reason given for not becoming a U.S. citizen is perhaps the most difficult to address. Approximately 20 percent of the non-citizen respondents reported that discrimination against Latinos in the United States was an important reason for not seeking naturalization, because discrimination colors their beliefs about the value of U.S. citizenship. This finding, however, does reflect a social reality of the nation. Public opinion polls that measure non-Latino Americans' attitudes towards Latinos, as well as negative images in the media and stereotypes in motion pictures, all reflect the reality that Latinos still encounter discrimination in this country (Smith 1990; National Conference 1994).

The conventional wisdom that Latino immigrants do not naturalize because they are attached to their home country was not substantiated by this study. In fact, just 13 percent of the non-citizen respondents mentioned loyalty to the home country as a reason for not naturalizing. Only one out of ten non-citizens saw mistreatment by the INS as an important reason for not becoming a citizen.

Latino National Origin Variations in Naturalization

In our discussion so far, we have examined Latino immigrants as a whole and have not distinguished among the experiences and attitudes of Latino national origin groups, for example Mexican Americans, Cuban Americans, or Dominican Americans. An extensive body of literature highlights the heterogeneous nature of Latino immigrant ethnicity (Portes and Bach 1985; Portes and Rumbaut 1990; de la Garza et al. 1992; Lamphere 1992; de la Garza, Menchaca, and DeSipio 1994). While the NLIS echoes these findings in terms of variations in demographic characteristics, home-country experiences, immigration and settlement patterns, and economic attainment in the United States, the survey also uncovers a common set of attitudes towards naturalization and a common difficulty with naturalization requirements and procedures. As we will indicate in the next chapter, we disaggregate the survey data by national origin in chapters three through six. Our decision to present these data in terms of national origin indicates the centrality with which we view national origin in any discussion of Latino immigrants.

While Latino immigrants from different parts of Latin America and the Caribbean were shaped by different experiences, the heterogeneity of their responses was less marked on core questions about attitudes toward naturalization. Ranging from a low of 93 percent among South Americans to a high of 100 percent among Dominicans, Latino immigrants planned to make the United States their permanent home. Between 68 and 85 percent reported that life was better in the United States than in the country of origin. Finally, between 81 percent (Central American immigrants) and 96 percent (Dominican immigrants) reported that becoming a U.S. citizen was either very or somewhat important. Thus, regardless of national origin, Latino immigrants saw the United States as their permanent home and saw U.S. citizenship as an important value. Yet when it came to putting this belief into practice, groups varied widely in their behavior. At one extreme, 78 percent of Cuban immigrants had initiated or completed naturalization. At the other extreme, just 52 percent of Mexican immigrants had begun or completed the requirements for naturalization. We will present some possible explanations for these variations in subsequent chapters.

The findings of the NALEO National Latino Immigrant Survey need to be examined with care. Simple generalizations about Latino immigrants are contradicted by our data. Latino immigrants are not a homogeneous group with uniform experiences and attitudes. Instead, Latino immigrants are heterogeneous and show a complexity of attitudes and experiences. In this regard, they mirror our nation's native-born Latino population. Regardless of this complexity, the NLIS offers evidence that the conventional wisdoms about Latino naturalization at the inception of this project do not accurately portray this population. Instead, Latino legal immigrants with the five years of residence necessary to naturalize planned to spend the rest of their lives in the United States and saw U.S. citizenship as important. The majority had taken some concrete action to achieve this goal. Yet, despite their interest, just half of those who had sought citizenship had accomplished their goal. Thus, Latino immigrants, like generations of immigrants before them, are seeking political incorporation. The degree to which the country and Latino leaders respond to this call will shape the future relationship between Latinos and the polity.

Conclusion

As of this writing, U.S. naturalization policy is in a state of flux. Due in part to the publicized findings of the NLIS and the activities of the NALEO Educational Fund, the newly appointed commissioner of the Immigration and Naturalization Service has committed the agency to a new campaign to promote naturalization among eligible immigrants and to provide resources to immigrant community organizations that assist immigrants. As the data presented in subsequent chapters will indicate, if the INS is successful in this initiative, it could have a sustained and positive impact on Latino naturalization rates.

At a time when our society is increasingly concerned about the lack of political participation among Americans as a whole, the promise of increased popular and policymaker awareness of naturalization is an important public policy objective. In 1990, there were more than ten million immigrants living in the United States who had not become citizens. The presence of these non-citizens in the polity raises two questions. Should

American society take a more active role in promoting the duties and responsibilities of American citizenship to these millions of people? Is the present INS policy of promoting American citizenship appropriate? Answers to these questions will vary, but our survey suggests that community education to promote the value of U.S. citizenship can be effective in increasing naturalization among the largest group of non-citizens in this country.

References

Bach, Robert. 1991. "Settlement Policies in the United States." In Gary P. Freeman and James Jupp, eds. *Nations of Immigrants: Australia, the United States, and International Migration*, pp. 145–164. Melbourne: Cambridge University Press.

Barnes, Fred. 1993. "No Entry: The Republicans' Immigration War." *The New Republic* (November 8): 10–14.

Carpenter, N. 1927. *Immigrants and their Children 1920*. New York: Arno Press.

de la Garza, Rodolfo O., and Louis DeSipio. 1993. "Save the Baby, Change the Bathwater, and Scrub the Tub: Latino Electoral Participation After Seventeen Years of Voting Rights Act Coverage." *Texas Law Review* 71 (7): 1479–1539.

de la Garza, Rodolfo O.; Louis DeSipio; F. Chris Garcia; John A. Garcia; and Angelo Falcon. 1992. *Latino Voices: Mexican, Puerto Rican, and Cuban Perspectives on American Politics*. Boulder, CO: Westview Press.

de la Garza, Rodolfo O.; Martha Menchaca; and Louis DeSipio. 1994. *Barrio Ballots: Latino Politics in the 1990 Elections*. Boulder, CO: Westview Press.

Decker, Cathleen. 1992. "Buchanan Uses Whatever It Takes in Long-Shot Bid." *The Los Angeles Times* (January 14).

DeSipio, Louis. 1987. "Social Science Literature and the Naturalization Process." *International Migration Review* 21 (78) (Summer): 390–405.

———. 1993. "Counting on the Latino Vote: Latinos as a New Electorate." Ph.D. dissertation, University of Texas at Austin.

DeSipio, Louis, and Harry P. Pachon. 1992. "Making Americans: Administrative Discretion and Americanization." *Chicano-Latino Law Review* 12 (Spring): 52–66.

DeSipio, Louis, and Rodolfo O. de la Garza. 1992. "Making Them Us: The Political Incorporation of Immigrant and Non-Immigrant Minorities in the United States." In Gary P. Freeman and James Jupp, eds. *Nations of Immigrants: Australia, the United States, and International Migration*, pp. 202–216. Melbourne: Cambridge University Press.

Duarte, E. B. 1985. "Role of the INS in Naturalization Outreach." In NALEO Educational Fund. *Proceedings of the First National Conference on Citizenship and the Hispanic Community*, pp. 16–17. Washington, D.C.: NALEO Educational Fund.

Erie, Steven P. 1988. *Rainbow's End: Irish Americans and the Dilemmas of Urban Machine Politics, 1840–1985*. Berkeley and Los Angeles: University of California Press.

Fuchs, Lawrence. 1990. *The American Kaleidoscope: Race, Ethnicity, and the Civic Culture*. Hanover, N.H.: The University Press of New England.

Freedman, Jonathan. 1994. "Wilson's New Witch Hunt: Prenatal Aliens." *The Los Angeles Times* (January 30).

Garcia, John. 1987. "The Political Integration of Mexican Immigrants: Examining Some Political Orientations." *International Migration Review* 21 (78) (Summer): 372–389.

Garza, Melita Marie. 1993. "Gutierrez-Sponsored Bill Seeks Funds for Immigrants' Classes." *The Chicago Tribune* (November 10).

Gavitt, John Palmer. 1971 (1922). *Americans by Choice*. Americanization Series 8. The Acculturation of Immigrant Groups into American Society. Montclair, N.J.: Patterson Smith.

Guest, A. M. 1980. "The Old-New Distinction and Naturalization 1900." *International Migration Review* 14 (4) (Winter): 492–510.

Hamilton, William. 1993. "Harvest of Blame: Californians Turn on Illegal Immigrants." *The Washington Post* (June 4).

Handlin, Oscar. 1951. *The Uprooted: The Epic Story of the Great Migrations that Made the American People*. New York: Little Brown and Company.

"Immigration Control: Doing It Right." 1993. *The Los Angeles Times* (August 29).

Kiely, Kathy. 1993. "Acting INS Chief Lists Efforts to Control Influx of Illegals." *The Houston Post* (September 30).

Lamphere, Louise. 1992. *Structuring Diversity: Ethnographic Perspectives on the New Immigration*. Chicago: The University of Chicago Press.

Mydans, Seth. 1993. "A New Tide of Immigration Brings Hostility to the Surface, Poll Finds." *The New York Times* (June 27).

Myers, Gustavus. 1968 [1917]. *The History of Tammany Hall*. New York: Burt Franklin.

NALEO. 1985. *Proceedings of the First National Conference on Citizenship and the Hispanic Community*. Washington, D.C.: NALEO Educational Fund.

———. 1993. "Seventy Congressional Districts Have 100,000 or More Latino Constituents." Washington, D.C.: NALEO Educational Fund.

National Conference. 1994. *Taking America's Pulse: The Full Report of the National Conference Survey on Inter-Group Relations*. New York: The National Conference.

Pachon, Harry P. 1987. "An Overview of Citizenship in the Hispanic Community." *International Migration Review* 21 (78) (Summer): 299–310.

———. 1991. "U.S. Citizenship and Latino Participation in California Politics." In Bryan O. Jackson and Michael B. Preston, eds. *Racial and Ethnic Politics in California*, pp. 71–88. Berkeley, CA: Institute of Governmental Studies Press.

Pachon, Harry P., and Louis DeSipio. 1992. "Latino Elected Officials in the 1990s." *PS Political Science & Politics* 25 (2) (June): 212–217.

Pachon, Harry P., and Lourdes Arguelles. 1994. "Grass-Roots Politics in an East Los Angeles Barrio: A Political Ethnography of the 1990 General Election." In Rodolfo O. de la Garza; Martha Menchaca; and Louis DeSipio, eds. *Barrio Ballots: Latino Politics in the 1990 Elections*, pp. 137–160. Boulder, CO: Westview Press.

Passel, Jeffrey S., and Barry Edmonston. 1991. "Immigration and Race: Recent Trends in Immigration to the United States." Paper prepared for presentation at the conference on "Immigration and Ethnicity: The Integration of America's Newest Immigrants," The Urban Institute, June 17–18.

Pear, Robert. 1993. "U.S. to Encourage Legal Immigrants to Get Citizenship." *The New York Times* (November 26).

Peel, Roy V. 1935. *The Political Clubs of New York City*. New York: G.P. Putnam's Sons.

Pierce, Neal R. 1993. "Immigration Dilemma Won't Go Away." *The National Journal* (June 5): 1367.

Portes, Alejandro, and John Curtis. 1987. "Changing Flags: Naturalization and its Determinants Among Mexican Immigrants." *International Migration Review* 21 (78) (Summer): 352–371.

Portes, Alejandro, and Robert Bach. 1985. *Latin Journey: Cuban and Mexican Immigrants in the United States*. Berkeley and Los Angeles: University of California Press.

Portes, Alejandro, and Ruben Rumbaut. 1990. *Immigrant America: A Portrait*. Berkeley and Los Angeles: University of California Press.

Pressley, Sue Ann. 1993. "On the Streets of El Paso, They're Feeling the Pinch." *The Washington Post* (November 14).

Rohter, Larry. 1994. "Florida Opens New Front in Fight on Immigrant Policy." *The New York Times* (February 11).

Schneider, William. 1993. "Americans Turn Against Immigration." *The National Journal* (July 24): 1900.

Simon, Jim, and Ross Ramsey. 1994. "U.S. Troops Should Patrol Border, Mattox Says." *The Houston Chronicle* (January 5).

Smith, Tom. 1990. "Ethnic Survey." *GSS Topical Report Number 19*. National Opinion Research Center. Chicago: University of Chicago, National Opinion Research Center.

U.S. Bureau of the Census. 1991a. "Race and Hispanic Origin" *1990 Census Profile* (2): June.

———. 1991b. "Census Bureau Releases Preliminary Coverage Estimates From the Post-Enumeration Survey Demographic Analysis." Press Release (April 18).

———. 1993a. *1990: The Foreign Born Population by Race, Hispanic Origin, and Citizenship for the United States and States*. CPH-L-134. Washington, D.C.: U.S. Bureau of the Census, Ethnic and Hispanic Branch.

———. 1993b. *Voting and Registration in the Election of November 1992*. Current Population Reports, Population Characteristics. Series P-20 #466. Washington, D.C.: U.S. Government Printing Office.

———. 1993c. "Table 4A. Reported Voting and Registration by Race, Hispanic Origin, and Age for States: November 1992." Unpublished Data. Washington, D.C.: Bureau of the Census.

———. 1993d. *Statistical Abstract of the United States 1993* (113th Edition). Washington, D.C.: U.S. Government Printing Office.

U.S. Immigration and Naturalization Service. 1988. *Statistical Yearbook of the Immigration and Naturalization Service, 1987*. Washington, D.C.: U.S. Government Printing Office.

———. 1992. *Statistical Yearbook of the Immigration and Naturalization Service, 1991*. Washington, D.C.: U.S. Government Printing Office.

———. 1993. *Statistical Yearbook of the Immigration and Naturalization Service, 1992*. Washington, D.C.: U.S. Government Printing Office.

Notes

1. We use the terms Latino and Hispanic interchangeably to refer to persons in the United States who can trace their ancestry to the Spanish-speaking regions of Latin America and the Caribbean.

2. There is one exception: naturalized citizens may not serve as president or vice president.

3. The first scholar to note the attachment to the United States of the "new" turn-of-century immigrants was John Palmer Gavitt (1971 [1922]). We recognize his scholarship by adapting the title of his major study—*Americans by Choice.*

4. Developing estimates of the size of the Latino and other immigrant populations and then the subset of the immigrant population eligible for naturalization is confounded by several factors. While the Immigration and Naturalization Service collects data on the number of immigrants to permanent residence, it does not maintain data on emigration or mortality of permanent residents. The census includes citizenship status in both its decennial enumeration and current population survey estimates. These census counts of non-citizens, however, include undocumented residents who are not eligible for naturalization and suffer from an undercount of between 4.4 and 7.9 percent by the Bureau's own estimates (U.S. Bureau of the Census 1991*b*). The undercount confounds the development of an estimate further because we would hypothesize that the undercount is not spread evenly among Latinos, but is more likely to reduce the count of the immigrant population. For a more complete discussion of the difficulties of enumerating the Latino legal immigrant population eligible for naturalization, see DeSipio (1993: 205–220).

2

Using the National Latino Immigrant Survey

The chapters that follow have a common format. The core of each chapter is a set of tables linked by a common theme. We begin each chapter with a synopsis of what we consider to be the most salient findings. This brief introduction also includes a list of the questions used to derive the tables presented in that section. The exact wording of the English version of the questionnaire appears in Appendix One. Where there are comparable data, we also present a list of tables from *Latino Voices: Mexican, Puerto Rican, and Cuban Perspectives on American Politics* (de la Garza et al. 1992). *Latino Voices* offers a wealth of comparative data for native-born Latinos and for Puerto Ricans, who were not a part of the National Latino Immigrant Survey sample. Throughout the volume, we keep the description to a minimum because we believe that the tables speak largely for themselves.

In order to interpret these tables accurately, it is necessary to take two factors into account, which we discuss in this chapter. First, we briefly review the survey population, so that it is clear who is and is not being discussed in these tables. Then, we offer some tips on how to read the tables. It is important to note that for each table, the reader should not only examine the range of answers but also observe who is being asked the question.

The Survey Population

All references to Latino immigrants are to Latino permanent resident immigrants who were eligible for U.S. citizenship or who had naturalized. Those eligible for U.S. citizenship included immigrants who had had a permanent resident visa for five years or who had been married to a U.S. citizen for three years. In this latter case, the U.S. citizen spouse had to have been a citizen for three years.

The sampling frame for NLIS respondents excluded some types of Latino immigrants as well as all native-born Latinos. Among the categories of excluded immigrants were: the undocumented; legal residents with fewer than five years of legal residence; and temporary visitors. For reasons explored in Appendix Two, the NLIS limited its sample to immigrants living in those counties where 80 percent of the Latino foreign-born population resided in 1980. These counties are areas with large populations of Latino immigrants and, as a result, are more urban than rural. Finally, the NLIS excluded people born in Puerto Rico, who are U.S. citizens by birth. As mentioned previously, a separate study—*Latino Voices*—offers comparative data, particularly on population demographics, on native-born Latinos, and on Puerto Ricans.

Within the Latino population, there is no precise estimate of what percentage is foreign-born adults with five years of legal residence or what percentage is naturalized (DeSipio 1993: 205-220). We do, however, know the size of the naturalized Latino population. The 1990 census (conducted approximately one and one half years after the NLIS) documented that of the total Latino population of 22.4 million, approximately 7.8 million or 35.1 percent were foreign-born. Of these 7.8 million foreign-born Latinos, 2.1 million (26.2 percent) had naturalized (U.S. Bureau of the Census 1991*a*: 4-5; 1993*a*: Table 1).

Among adult Latinos, the share of non-U.S. citizens is even higher. Of the 14.7 million adult Latinos in 1992, 5.9 million or 40.2 percent were not citizens (U.S. Bureau of the Census 1993*b*: Table 2). There are no data publicly available from the Census Bureau on the share of the 1992 Latino adult population who were naturalized.

Not all of the foreign-born non-citizens (and non-citizen adults), however, were eligible for inclusion in the NLIS. Those with fewer than five years of legal residence were statutorily excluded from naturalization and, as a result, excluded from the NLIS sampling frame so as to limit its focus to those who could naturalize if they so chose. Again, it is not possible to provide a population estimate of the share of the Latino adult non-citizen population comprised of these recent arrivals. According to the 1990 census, the eleven countries in Latin America with the largest number of their nationals residing in the United States constituted more than 90 percent of Latino immigrants in the United States. Of those residing in the United States who were born in these eleven countries, approximately 27 percent had resided in the United States for less than five years (U.S. Bureau of the Census 1993*c*: Table 1).

The next limitation on developing an estimate of the Latino immigrant population who had naturalized or were eligible for naturalization results from the Census Bureau's decision not to collect data on an individual's legal status. As a result, it is not possible to estimate the number of undocumented immigrants among the Latino population.

A final limitation on developing an accurate count of the number of Latino foreign-born adults eligible for naturalization is due to the census undercount of the Latino population of between 973,000 and 1,764,000 people (U.S. Bureau of the Census 1991*b*). While we assume that undocumented immigrants and recently arrived permanent residents would be more likely than the citizenship-eligible and the naturalized to be neglected by the census, the undercount reduces our ability to develop an accurate estimate of the size of the citizenship-eligible population.

With these limitations in mind, our best estimate is that the Latino citizenship-eligible population numbered between 3.25 and 3.75 million at the time of the survey. These citizenship-eligible Latinos add to the approximately 2.1 million naturalized Latinos to constitute the Latino foreign-born population with five or more years of residence. The best estimate is that between 70 and 75 percent of these naturalized- and citizenship-eligible Latino immigrants were adults.

Central and South Americans: Aggregate Responses May Mask National Origin Differences

The size of the NLIS sample assures that we can present detailed data on the three largest Latino immigrant populations—Mexican Americans, Cuban Americans, and Dominican Americans. The sample also included Latino immigrants from elsewhere in Latin America. No individual country in this region provided sufficient numbers of respondents to report on specific national origin characteristics. We do, however, provide aggregate responses for Central American and South American immigrants. Presenting data in this manner does not imply that we believe that all Central Americans or all South Americans shared similar demographic characteristics, immigration or naturalization experiences, or political attitudes and behaviors. Instead, we present these data in order to compare and contrast these "other" Latino characteristics and experiences with those of the more sizable Latino national origin groups.

How to Read the Tables

The tables follow a common format. All are based on weighted data (see Appendix Two). The first number in the cell indicates the number of respondents of the given characteristic (the column) answering the question in the given way (the row). The characteristic (or column) in chapters 3 through 6 is national origin, stage in the naturalization process in chapter 7, and state of residence in chapter 8. The second figure is a percentage of those answering the question who answered in the stated way. The sum at the bottom of each column represents the total number of respondents of the given characteristic who answered the question. Thus, in Table 2.1, 141 respondents from Mexico had one generation living in the household. These respondents represented 20.5 percent of the 686 respondents from Mexico who answered the question about people in the household.

The reader should note not only the distribution of the answers among the options given, but also the total number of respondents from each national origin group that answered the question. If all respondents answered a question, then there would be 709 responses from Mexico, 429 responses from Cuba, 110 responses from the Dominican Republic, 172 from Central America, and 216 from South America. In many cases, however, either not all respondents were asked a given question or not all chose to answer the question. An example of the first type of non-response is questions about experience with the naturalization exam (Tables 6.32 to 6.44). We asked these questions only of respondents who indicated that they had taken the citizenship exam. There is no pattern to the second type of non-response—respondents simply chose not to answer certain types of questions. The questions with the highest level of voluntary non-response asked about household income in the previous month (questions 105-107; Table 3.17 and 3.18). Approximately 11 percent of respondents refused to answer these questions.

In chapter seven, we report on the demographic characteristics, political attitudes and behaviors, and immigration and naturalization experiences of Latino immigrants by stage in the naturalization process. In this chapter, the number of respondents in the initial stage—those who had

TABLE 2.1 Generations Living in Household, by National Origin

Generations Living in Household	*Mexico*	*Cuba*	*Dominican Republic*	*Central America*	*South America*
One	141 20.5%	154 39.9%	16 15.3%	46 28.8%	47 24.3%
Two	502 73.1%	182 47.1%	77 76.2%	96 61.0%	138 72.0%
Three	44 6.4%	50 13.0%	9 8.6%	16 10.2%	7 3.7%
Column total	686 100.0%	387 100.0%	102 100.0%	158 100.0%	192 100.0%

not initiated the naturalization process—was 600. Those who had initiated but not completed the process numbered 453. Four hundred nine respondents had naturalized. For reasons that we will discuss in chapter seven, we exclude 174 respondents from this analysis. These individuals naturalized as part of their parents' naturalizations and did not necessarily experience the naturalization process.

In chapter eight, we examine respondent characteristics and responses by state for the four states with the largest number of Latino immigrants. These states—California, Florida, New York, and Texas—have 432, 335, 281, and 340 respondents, respectively. This state-focused analysis excludes the 248 respondents who resided outside of these four states.

In some cases, we combine interrelated questions into a single table. In these cases, respondents had the option of selecting more than one answer. For example, in Table 4.8, respondents may have been members of more than one type of community organization. In these types of tables, we present the total number of respondents answering the question in each cell.

As mentioned above, the data presented in these tables are weighted so as to represent the national population of Latino immigrants who were statutorily eligible for naturalization or who had naturalized. The percentages in each cell are the true weighted proportion of respondents in the national population answering the particular question in the manner indicated. For the sake of clarity, we present rounded whole numbers to indicate the respondents in each cell. Thus, in Table 2.1, the number of respondents from Mexico indicating that one generation resided in their household ranged from 140.5 to 141.49. The calculation of percentages based on weighted values explains the seemingly anomalous situation of cell values of zero having a non-zero percentage or of the whole number values in the cells not summing to the column total. An example of this first situation can be seen in the case of South Americans with four children in Table 3.8. The second appears among respondents from Mexico and Cuba in Table 2.1.

References

de la Garza, Rodolfo O.; Louis DeSipio; F. Chris Garcia; John A. Garcia; and Angelo Falcon. 1992. *Latino Voices: Mexican, Puerto Rican, and Cuban Perspectives on American Politics*. Boulder, CO: Westview Press.

DeSipio, Louis. 1993. "Counting on the Latino Vote: Latinos as a New Electorate." Ph.D. Dissertation, University of Texas at Austin.

U.S. Bureau of the Census. 1991a. "Race and Hispanic Origin." *1990 Census Profile 2* (June).

———. 1991b. "Census Bureau Releases Preliminary Coverage Estimates from the Post-Enumeration Survey Demographic Analysis." Press Release (April 18).

———. 1993a. *1990: The Foreign Born Population by Race, Hispanic Origin, and Citizenship for the United States and States*. CPH-L-134. Washington, D.C.: Ethnic and Hispanic Branch, Population Division.

———. 1993b. *Voting and Registration in the Election of November 1992*. Current Population Reports. Population Characteristics. P20–466. Washington, D.C.: U.S. Government Printing Office.

———. 1993c. *1990 Census of Population: The Foreign Born Population of the United States*. CP–3-1. Washington, D.C.: U.S. Government Printing Office.

3

Social and Demographic Characteristics of Latino Immigrants with Five or More Years of Permanent Residence

This chapter offers a portrait of the respondents to the National Latino Immigrant Survey. These data allow the interested reader to compare the NLIS sample with available census and Immigration and Naturalization Service data in order to evaluate the quality of the sample. This chapter also presents background information for evaluating the characteristics of the people whose attitudes and behaviors we discuss in the next five chapters. The data presented in this chapter should accent the need to examine the characteristics of *individual* Latino national origin groups as well as to explore their collective experiences. We divide our discussion into four parts: (1) personal, familial, and household demographics; (2) education, income, employment, and housing; (3) language abilities; and (4) immigration and citizenship experiences.

Personal, Familial, and Household Demographic Characteristics

Findings

Latino immigrants eligible for naturalization were more likely to be women than men (Table 3.1). This pattern was particularly evident among Dominican immigrants.

On average, Cuban immigrants were older than the other Latin American immigrants, with 46 percent aged fifty-one or older (Table 3.2). Mexican and Central American immigrants, on the other hand, were the youngest of the Latino immigrants.

Mexican immigrants were the most likely to be married (Table 3.3). With the exception of Central Americans, who were the most likely to report having never been married, however, all of the national origin groups reported high marriage rates.

Respondents were likely to marry people of the same national origin (co-nationals) as themselves (Table 3.4). Only Mexican and Central American immigrants had a high propensity to marry non-co-nationals. These non-co-nationals, mostly people born in the United States, could have been people of the same ancestry born in the United States. Cuban immigrants were the least likely to marry non-Cubans.

More than two-thirds of all Latino immigrants had children living in the United States (Table 3.5). Mexicans and Dominicans were the most likely to have children in the United States and Central Americans the least likely.

Most Latino immigrant households had two generations residing in them (Table 3.6). The most frequent pattern was an immigrant as well as his or her children. Cuban immigrant households showed the most diversity. Nearly 40 percent were single-generation households and 13 percent held three generations, with the most common three-generation pattern being the immigrant, his or her parent(s), and his or her children.

Dominican households had the fewest number of resident adults (Table 3.7). Slightly more than 26 percent had three or more adults compared to 45 percent for Cuban immigrant households and slightly more than 35 percent for Mexican, Central American, and South American households.

Cubans were the most likely of the Latino immigrants not to have any children residing in the household (Table 3.8). Mexican immigrants, on the other hand, were more than twice as likely as other Latino immigrant groups to have three or more children residing at home.

The majority of the children residing in Latino immigrant households were born in the United States (Table 3.9). Nativity in the United States grants U.S. citizenship regardless of the citizenship of the parents. Between 17 and 36 percent of Latino immigrant households had children who were born abroad. Foreign-born children were most common in Dominican and Central American households and were least likely in Mexican and Cuban households.

Mexican immigrant households had the most members and Cuban households the fewest (Table 3.10). Nearly 40 percent of Mexican households had five or more members compared to just 16 percent of Cuban immigrant households. At the other extreme, 41 percent of Cuban households had one or two members. The comparable figures for small households among Mexican, Dominican, Central American, and South American households were 18, 24, 29, and 26 percent, respectively.

Questions Asked: E, F, G, H, I, J, N, P, Q, 35, and 41.
Tables with Comparable Data in Latino Voices: 2.1, 2.3, 2.4, 2.6, 2.7, 3.1, 3.3, 3.4, 3.6, 3.8, 10.1, 10.3, 10.4, and 10.6.

TABLE 3.1 Gender, by National Origin

Gender	*Mexico*	*Cuba*	*Dominican Republic*	*Central America*	*South America*
Female	391 55.1%	258 60.1%	79 71.5%	103 59.6%	110 51.1%
Male	318 44.9%	171 39.9%	32 28.5%	70 40.4%	105 48.9%
Total	709 100.0%	429 100.0%	110 100.0%	172 100.0%	216 100.0%

TABLE 3.2 Age, by National Origin

Age	*Mexico*	*Cuba*	*Dominican Republic*	*Central America*	*South America*
18-24	86 12.1%	53 12.4%	3 2.7%	30 17.3%	18 8.2%
25-34	223 31.4%	54 12.5%	34 31.2%	47 27.3%	60 27.9%
35-50	251 35.4%	124 28.9%	49 44.3%	56 32.5%	110 51.0%
51-65	87 12.3%	126 29.3%	20 18.3%	22 12.8%	16 7.3%
66 or older	62 8.8%	73 16.9%	4 3.4%	18 10.2%	12 5.6%
Total	709 100.0%	429 100.0%	110 100.0%	172 100.0%	216 100.0%

TABLE 3.3 Current Marital Status, by National Origin

Current Marital Status	*Mexico*	*Cuba*	*Dominican Republic*	*Central America*	*South America*
Married	516 72.9%	286 66.6%	72 65.5%	80 46.3%	140 64.7%
Separated	24 3.4%	15 3.4%	12 10.9%	17 9.6%	8 3.6%
Divorced	28 3.9%	45 10.5%	19 17.0%	19 10.8%	27 12.6%
Widowed	37 5.2%	19 4.5%	5 4.7%	3 1.9%	11 5.0%
Never married	103 14.6%	64 15.0%	2 1.9%	54 31.3%	30 14.0%
Total	708 100.0%	428 100.0%	110 100.0%	172 100.0%	216 100.0%

TABLE 3.4 National Origin of Spouse, by National Origin

National Origin of Spouse	*Mexico*	*Cuba*	*Dominican Republic*	*Central America*	*South America*
Same as respondent	336 49.8%	226 58.7%	37 39.0%	43 26.0%	81 42.0%
The United States	125 18.5%	11 3.0%	10 9.9%	17 10.4%	19 9.9%
Latin American country other than respondent's	14 2.0%	12 3.2%	2 1.8%	10 5.8%	10 5.4%
Other	5 0.7%	7 1.7%	7 7.1%	2 0.9%	13 6.8%
No spouse	195 28.9%	128 33.3%	40 42.2%	94 56.9%	69 35.8%
Total	675 100.0%	385 100.0%	96 100.0%	165 100.0%	192 100.0%

TABLE 3.5 Children Living in the United States, by National Origin

Children Living in the United States	*Mexico*	*Cuba*	*Dominican Republic*	*Central America*	*South America*
Yes	582 82.2%	309 72.1%	90 81.5%	114 66.3%	158 73.2%
No	126 17.8%	120 27.9%	20 18.5%	58 33.7%	58 26.8%
Total	709 100.0%	429 100.0%	110 100.0%	172 100.0%	216 100.0%

TABLE 3.6 Generations Living in Household, by National Origin

Generations Living in Household	*Mexico*	*Cuba*	*Dominican Republic*	*Central America*	*South America*
One	141 20.5%	154 39.9%	16 15.3%	46 28.8%	47 24.3%
Two	502 73.1%	182 47.1%	77 76.2%	96 61.0%	138 72.0%
Three	44 6.4%	50 13.0%	9 8.6%	16 10.2%	7 3.7%
Total	686 100.0%	387 100.0%	102 100.0%	158 100.0%	192 100.0%

TABLE 3.7 Number of Adults Living in Household, by National Origin

Number of Adults Living in Household	*Mexico*	*Cuba*	*Dominican Republic*	*Central America*	*South America*
One	77 11.3%	44 10.9%	16 15.2%	31 19.5%	18 9.4%
Two	360 52.5%	178 44.1%	61 58.4%	70 44.7%	103 53.6%
Three	88 12.9%	79 19.7%	17 16.4%	25 15.7%	29 14.9%
Four	107 15.7%	82 20.4%	9 8.5%	27 17.6%	32 16.7%
Five or more	53 7.7%	20 4.9%	2 1.5%	4 2.5%	10 5.4%
Total	686 100.0%	404 100.0%	105 100.0%	156 100.0%	193 100.0%

TABLE 3.8 Number of Children Living in Household, by National Origin

Number of Children Living in Household	*Mexico*	*Cuba*	*Dominican Republic*	*Central America*	*South America*
No Children in Household	223 32.5%	275 70.8%	27 26.5%	60 38.0%	71 36.9%
One	140 20.4%	60 15.4%	34 33.8%	35 22.3%	64 33.3%
Two	148 21.6%	35 8.9%	27 26.9%	48 30.1%	41 21.3%
Three	119 17.4%	17 4.3%	10 10.1%	12 7.4%	15 7.6%
Four	34 4.9%	3 0.7%	3 2.7%	2 1.6%	1 0.7%
Five or more	22 3.1%	0 0.0%	0 0.0%	1 0.7%	0 0.2%
Total	685 100.0%	389 100.0%	102 100.0%	158 100.0%	192 100.0%

TABLE 3.9 Nativity of Children in Household, by National Origin

Nativity of Children Living in Household	*Mexico*	*Cuba*	*Dominican Republic*	*Central America*	*South America*
The United States	355 77.0%	94 83.1%	47 63.9%	64 64.9%	89 73.2%
Abroad	29 6.3%	14 12.4%	17 23.4%	21 21.8%	20 16.6%
Mixed U.S. and Abroad	77 16.8%	5 4.5%	9 12.7%	13 13.3%	12 10.2%
Total	462 100.0%	113 100.0%	74 100.0%	98 100.0%	121 100.0%

TABLE 3.10 Total Number of Household Residents, by National Origin

Household Size	*Mexico*	*Cuba*	*Dominican Republic*	*Central America*	*South America*
One	39 5.7%	39 10.1%	3 2.6%	21 13.1%	14 7.4%
Two	84 12.3%	121 31.1%	22 21.7%	25 15.8%	36 18.6%
Three	116 16.9%	74 19.0%	28 27.6%	18 11.6%	46 23.9%
Four	173 25.3%	92 23.7%	25 24.8%	58 37.3%	51 26.5%
Five or more	272 39.8%	63 16.1%	24 23.4%	35 22.1%	45 23.6%
Total	683 100.0%	387 100.0%	102 100.0%	156 100.0%	192 100.0%

Education, Income, Employment, and Housing

Findings

More than half of Mexican and Dominican immigrants had eight or fewer years of formal education (Table 3.11). At the other extreme, more than half of Central American and South American immigrants had earned high school degrees or had studied beyond the high school level. Nearly half of Cuban immigrants held a high school degree.

The majority of Latino immigrants earned their highest degree abroad (Table 3.12). This pattern was particularly evident among Dominican immigrants, among whom more than three-quarters of those with a degree earned it abroad.

Respondents' spouses followed the same patterns relating to level of education and country of education as the respondents (Tables 3.13 and 3.14). Half of the spouses of Mexican immigrants and nearly half of the spouses of Dominican respondents had eight or fewer years of education. More than 40 percent of the spouses of Central Americans and South Americans had a high school degree or had studied beyond the high school level. The majority of spouses earned their highest degree abroad.

Overall, Mexican respondents and their spouses had the fewest years of combined level of education, with more than 40 percent reporting that both spouses had eight or fewer years of education (Table 3.15). Twenty-five percent or more of Dominican, Central American, and South American households had at least one spouse with post-high-school education.

Few Latino immigrants served in the all-volunteer United States Armed Forces (Table 3.16).

Household income levels varied among Latino national origin groups. More than 44 percent of the Dominican respondents reported household incomes of $9,600 or less for 1988 (Table 3.17). Approximately 25 percent of Mexican immigrant households had incomes at or below this level. In Central American and South American households, approximately 21 percent earned $9,600 or less. Cuban immigrant households had the lowest share in this poverty status, with just 18 percent reporting extremely low household incomes.

Few Latino immigrant households earned more than $30,000 per year. This higher level of household income was the average income for all families in the United States in 1988. Central American households were the most likely to have incomes at this level, with slightly more than 23 percent of respondents reporting income this high. Central American households were followed by South American, Cuban, Mexican, and Dominican households in terms of having incomes comparable to the average for all U.S. households in 1988.

These differences in earnings among the Latino national origin groups were reinforced when we examined per capita income for household adults (Table 3.18). More than 40 percent of Central American and 38 percent of South American households had per capita incomes exceeding $10,000 per year. At the other extreme, 43 percent of Dominican and 31 percent of Mexican immigrant households had per capita household incomes of $5,000 per year or less.

Among Latino immigrants who migrated as adults, the majority of each of the national origin group worked in the country of origin (Table 3.19). Central American immigrants showed the highest rates of home-country work and Dominican immigrants the lowest rates.

More than 90 percent of the respondents, regardless of national origin, had worked in the United States (Table 3.20). Dominican immigrants had the highest rates in this category.

Sizable minorities of Latino immigrants had faced six month or greater periods of unemployment in the United States (Table 3.21). South Americans were the least likely to have faced lengthy unemployment and Dominicans were the most likely.

Most Latino immigrants began their work history in the United States in full-time jobs (Table 3.22). The rates of full-time first jobs varied from 72 percent among Central Americans to 87 percent among Dominicans.

The industry of the first U.S. job for Latino immigrants was most likely to be manufacturing (Table 3.23). National-origin variations, however, appeared. Fully one-quarter of Mexican immigrants entered the U.S. workforce through agriculture compared to virtually none of the immigrants of the other Latino nationalities. More than one-quarter of Cubans began their U.S. work experience with jobs in trade. More than one-fifth of Dominicans also worked in trade. Almost one-quarter of Central Americans began to work in the United States in personal service.

The specific skills required in the first job among Latino immigrants were most likely to be those of operatives (Table 3.24). Again, variation appeared according to nationality. Nearly one-quarter of Mexicans served as farm laborers. One-fifth of Cubans performed clerical tasks. One-quarter of Dominicans and one-fifth of Central Americans and South Americans worked in the service occupations.

The majority of Latino immigrants were working full time (Table 3.25). Central Americans were most likely to be working full time. Dominicans were the most likely to be temporarily laid off and Cubans were the most likely not to be in the labor force.

At the time of the survey, respondents were most likely to be found in manufacturing industries (Table 3.26). Between the first job and the job at the time of the survey, the likelihood of finding Mexicans in agriculture declined by about one-half. The share of Cubans and Central Americans in professional industries doubled. The share of Dominicans in personal service increased while the share of Central Americans and South Americans in this industry declined. The number of Dominicans in agriculture also increased considerably.

Operatives was the most likely current job among Latino immigrants (Table 3.27). For all national origin groups except Mexicans, however, the share reporting operative job skills declined between the first job and the current job. The share of managers and professionals increased dramatically for all national origin groups.

Among Mexican and Cuban immigrants, more than 25 percent of respondents had worked for the same employer for eleven or more years (Table 3.28). The majority of Dominican, Central American, and South American immigrants and nearly a majority of Mexican immigrants had worked for their current employers for five years or less.

Few Latino immigrants reported dissatisfaction with their jobs (Table 3.29). Though low in numbers, South American immigrants were the most likely to be dissatisfied. Cuban respondents were not only the most likely to be satisfied, they were the most likely to report that they were "very" satisfied among those who reported general satisfaction.

Between 12 and 19 percent of respondents reported that they were working at more than one job (Table 3.30). The Cubans and Dominicans were the most likely to report this.

Regardless of the national origin of the respondent, more than 80 percent of their spouses had worked for pay in the United States (Table 3.31).

The majority of spouses worked full time (Table 3.32). Among Mexican and Cuban respondents, approximately two-thirds of the spouses were working full time. Among Dominican, Central American, and South American respondents, approximately three-quarters of the spouses were working full time.

The spouses were most likely to work in manufacturing industries (Table 3.33). Again, Mexican respondents' spouses were more likely to be found in agriculture than the spouses of other groups. The spouses of Dominicans and South Americans were more likely to be found in trade than were the spouses of the other nationalities.

The most common occupations among respondents' spouses were operative and craftsperson (Table 3.34). Dominicans' spouses were more likely to be found in the service occupations than were the spouses of the other groups.

Few Latino immigrants had received assistance from government benefit programs, whether contributory or need-based (Table 3.35). The three most common programs were Social Security, Medicare, and Medicaid. Slightly more than one-quarter of Dominicans had received Medicare or Medicaid. This rate of program use, however, was the highest for any of the programs among all the national origin groups.

More than half of Cuban and Mexican immigrants owned their own home (Table 3.36). Dominican immigrants, on the other hand, were much more likely to rent their home.

Among homeowners, the majority of Dominicans, Central Americans, and South Americans had purchased their home in the eight years prior to the survey (Table 3.37). Mexicans and Cubans, on the other hand, show significant patterns of home acquisition in the 1960s and 1970s as well as in the 1980s.

The majority of Mexican and Cuban immigrants reported having resided in the same area for eleven or more years (Table 3.38). The modal length of residence in the same area for Dominicans and South Americans was six to ten years and one to five years for Central Americans.

Questions Asked: E, 3, 15, 19, 20, 21, 22, 23, 24, 25, 26, 27, 30, 31, 32, 33, 34, 34a, 35, 36, 37, 38, 39, 40, 40a, 103, 105, 106, 107, and 108.
Tables with Comparable Data in Latino Voices: 2.8, 2.9, 2.11, 2.12, 2.18, 2.19, 2.20, 2.22, 2.17, 3.9, 3.10, 3.12, 3.13, 3.14, 3.15, 10.7, 10.8, 10.9, 10.11, 10.12, 10.13, and 10.14.

TABLE 3.11 Respondent's Education, by National Origin

Education	*Mexico*	*Cuba*	*Dominican Republic*	*Central America*	*South America*
0-8 years	392 55.2%	120 28.0%	63 57.2%	61 35.2%	42 19.5%
9-12 years, no degree	78 11.0%	98 22.9%	11 10.1%	25 14.4%	55 25.5%
High school graduate	171 24.1%	134 31.3%	19 17.5%	42 24.3%	76 35.2%
Beyond high school	68 9.6%	76 17.7%	17 15.2%	45 26.1%	43 19.7%
Total	709 100.0%	429 100.0%	110 100.0%	172 100.0%	216 100.0%

TABLE 3.12 Country Awarding Highest Degree, by National Origin

Country Where Highest Degree Earned	*Mexico*	*Cuba*	*Dominican Republic*	*Central America*	*South America*
United States	180 39.5%	125 38.9%	17 23.7%	67 49.2%	78 44.0%
Abroad	276 60.5%	196 61.1%	55 76.3%	70 50.8%	99 56.0%
Total	456 100.0%	321 100.0%	72 100.0%	137 100.0%	178 100.0%

TABLE 3.13 Spouse's Education, by National Origin

Spouse's Education	*Mexico*	*Cuba*	*Dominican Republic*	*Central America*	*South America*
0-8 years	226 50.6%	80 29.7%	29 46.2%	25 38.2%	26 20.0%
9-12 years, no degree	87 19.6%	97 36.2%	11 16.6%	12 18.6%	47 36.9%
High school graduate	102 22.9%	58 21.6%	16 24.9%	20 30.3%	36 28.2%
Beyond high school	31 6.9%	33 12.4%	8 12.3%	8 12.9%	19 15.0%
Total	446 100.0%	269 100.0%	64 100.0%	65 100.0%	128 100.0%

TABLE 3.14 Country Awarding Spouse's Highest Degree, by National Origin

Country Where Spouse's Highest Degree Earned	*Mexico*	*Cuba*	*Dominican Republic*	*Central America*	*South America*
United States	138 44.7%	55 28.0%	21 45.2%	24 37.4%	50 46.7%
Abroad	171 55.3%	142 72.0%	25 54.8%	40 62.6%	57 53.3%
Total	309 100.0%	197 100.0%	46 100.0%	64 100.0%	108 100.0%

TABLE 3.15 Combined Respondent and Spouse Education Levels, by National Origin

Combined Levels of Education, Respondent and Spouse	*Mexico*	*Cuba*	*Dominican Republic*	*Central America*	*South America*
0-8 years	175 40.3%	63 23.9%	20 33.7%	14 21.8%	7 5.2%
One 8 years or less, one 9-12 years	52 12.0%	15 5.8%	2 3.9%	3 5.3%	26 20.4%
Both 9-12 years, no degree	16 3.7%	41 15.6%	4 6.4%	2 2.9%	12 9.2%
One high school graduate, one less than high school graduate	85 19.5%	69 26.3%	14 23.1%	16 24.5%	32 25.0%
Both high school graduates	49 11.2%	27 10.4%	5 8.3%	12 18.9%	17 13.5%
One post-high-school, one high school graduate or less	45 10.5%	24 9.0%	10 16.4%	10 15.9%	20 16.1%
Both post-high-school	12 2.8%	23 8.8%	5 8.2%	7 10.6%	14 10.7%
Total	434 100.0%	263 100.0%	61 100.0%	65 100.0%	127 100.0%

TABLE 3.16 Service in the United States Armed Forces, by National Origin

Service in the United States Armed Forces	*Mexico*	*Cuba*	*Dominican Republic*	*Central America*	*South America*
Yes	13 1.8%	16 3.7%	0 0.4%	10 5.7%	7 3.2%
No	695 98.2%	413 96.3%	110 99.6%	162 94.3%	209 96.8%
Total	708 100.0%	429 100.0%	110 100.0%	172 100.0%	216 100.0%

TABLE 3.17 Yearly Household Income, by National Origin

Household Income (1988)	*Mexico*	*Cuba*	*Dominican Republic*	*Central America*	*South America*
Less than $6,000	73 10.3%	29 6.8%	23 20.7%	12 6.8%	10 4.5%
$6,000-$9,600	104 14.6%	48 11.3%	26 23.7%	25 14.5%	35 16.4%
$9,601-$14,400	116 16.4%	40 9.4%	16 14.9%	14 8.3%	22 10.0%
$14,401-$17,999	60 8.5%	51 11.9%	8 7.2%	11 6.5%	15 7.1%
$18,000-$24,000	120 16.9%	76 17.8%	19 17.1%	28 16.4%	43 20.2%
$24,001-$30,000	64 9.0%	65 15.2%	13 11.6%	15 8.9%	29 13.4%
$30,001-$36,000	48 6.8%	27 6.4%	2 1.9%	19 10.8%	14 6.6%
$36,001 or more	45 6.4%	40 9.4%	1 0.5%	21 12.3%	24 10.9%
Refused to answer	79 11.1%	51 11.9%	3 2.3%	27 15.5%	24 10.9%
Total	709 100.0%	429 100.0%	110 100.0%	172 100.0%	216 100.0%

TABLE 3.18 Per Capita Household Income, by National Origin

Per Capita Household Income (1988)	*Mexico*	*Cuba*	*Dominican Republic*	*Central America*	*South America*
$2,500 or less	76 11.1%	20 4.9%	16 15.1%	9 5.5%	8 4.2%
$2,501-$5,000	139 20.2%	73 17.8%	29 27.7%	21 13.4%	35 17.9%
$5,001-$10,000	197 28.5%	139 34.0%	32 30.6%	38 24.4%	54 28.1%
$10,001-$20,000	154 22.3%	100 24.6%	22 20.8%	56 35.4%	55 28.6%
$20,001 or more	44 6.4%	26 6.4%	3 3.3%	7 4.4%	17 9.0%
Refused to answer	79 11.4%	51 12.4%	3 2.5%	27 16.9%	24 12.2%
Total	690 100.0%	409 100.0%	105 100.0%	158 100.0%	193 100.0%

TABLE 3.19 Work Experience in Home Country Among Immigrants Who Emigrated as Adults, by National Origin

Did Respondent Work in the Country of Origin?	*Mexico*	*Cuba*	*Dominican Republic*	*Central America*	*South America*
Yes	243 58.8%	181 60.8%	50 53.3%	84 70.9%	104 62.6%
No	170 41.2%	117 39.2%	44 46.7%	35 29.1%	62 37.4%
Total	413 100.0%	298 100.0%	93 100.0%	119 100.0%	167 100.0%

TABLE 3.20 Work Experience in the United States, by National Origin

Did Respondent Work for Pay in the United States?	*Mexico*	*Cuba*	*Dominican Republic*	*Central America*	*South America*
Yes	639 90.2%	394 91.9%	108 97.6%	158 91.8%	196 90.7%
No	70 9.8%	35 8.1%	3 2.4%	14 8.2%	20 9.3%
Total	709 100.0%	429 100.0%	110 100.0%	172 100.0%	216 100.0%

TABLE 3.21 Period of Lengthy Unemployment in the United States, by National Origin

Did Respondent Have Unemployment of Six Months or More Since Migrating to the United States?	*Mexico*	*Cuba*	*Dominican Republic*	*Central America*	*South America*
Yes	173 27.1%	97 24.6%	48 44.7%	39 24.4%	33 16.8%
No	466 72.9%	297 75.4%	60 55.3%	120 75.6%	163 83.2%
Total	639 100.0%	394 100.0%	108 100.0%	158 100.0%	196 100.0%

TABLE 3.22 Work Level of First Job in the United States, by National Origin

Work Level of First Job in the United States	*Mexico*	*Cuba*	*Dominican Republic*	*Central America*	*South America*
Full-time	510 80.1%	307 77.9%	94 87.0%	113 71.7%	159 82.3%
Part-time	127 19.9%	87 22.1%	14 13.0%	45 28.3%	34 17.7%
Total	636 100.0%	394 100.0%	108 100.0%	158 100.0%	193 100.0%

TABLE 3.23 Industry of First Job in the United States, by National Origin

Industry of First Job	*Mexico*	*Cuba*	*Dominican Republic*	*Central America*	*South America*
Agriculture	163 25.7%	2 0.6%	0 0.0%	4 2.5%	0 0.0%
Construction	37 5.8%	15 4.0%	0 0.0%	11 6.9%	5 2.6%
Manufacturing	185 29.3%	137 36.3%	56 53.4%	45 29.3%	85 48.3%
Transportation/ communications	6 0.9%	11 2.9%	2 2.2%	9 6.1%	2 1.4%
Trade	101 15.9%	100 26.5%	23 21.8%	29 18.8%	31 17.4%
Finance	3 0.4%	19 5.1%	0 0.0%	3 2.3%	6 3.6%
Business	19 2.9%	23 6.2%	3 2.4%	5 3.2%	6 3.4%
Personal service	67 10.6%	36 9.6%	11 10.7%	34 22.4%	24 13.3%
Professional	35 5.5%	30 7.9%	4 3.9%	11 7.4%	15 8.8%
Other	18 2.9%	3 0.8%	6 5.6%	2 1.1%	2 1.3%
Total	632 100.0%	377 100.0%	105 100.0%	153 100.0%	177 100.0%

TABLE 3.24 First Occupation, by National Origin

Job Skills in First U.S. Job	*Mexico*	*Cuba*	*Dominican Republic*	*Central America*	*South America*
Household labor	32 5.2%	10 2.9%	10 9.9%	16 10.3%	9 5.0%
Service	91 14.6%	63 17.7%	27 25.9%	32 20.5%	37 20.3%
Farm labor	146 23.5%	2 0.4%	0 0.0%	2 1.5%	0 0.0%
Laborer	89 14.4%	26 7.4%	11 11.1%	16 10.7%	11 5.9%
Transport	7 1.1%	9 2.6%	1 1.1%	11 7.0%	0 0.0%
Operative	151 24.3%	110 31.0%	40 38.7%	32 20.8%	76 41.8%
Craftsperson	36 5.7%	37 10.3%	6 5.5%	7 4.7%	17 9.1%
Clerical	51 8.1%	73 20.6%	8 7.5%	20 13.2%	17 9.2%
Sales	10 1.7%	8 2.3%	0 0.0%	10 6.5%	7 3.7%
Manager	1 0.2%	4 1.0%	0 0.0%	1 0.7%	0 0.2%
Professional	8 1.3%	13 3.7%	0 0.4%	6 4.1%	9 4.9%
Total	621 100.0%	354 100.0%	103 100.0%	154 100.0%	182 100.0%

TABLE 3.25 Current Labor Force Status, by National Origin

Current Labor Force Status	*Mexico*	*Cuba*	*Dominican Republic*	*Central America*	*South America*
In labor force	393 55.4%	232 54.0%	60 54.7%	116 67.2%	136 63.1%
Temporarily unemployed	70 9.8%	37 8.5%	21 18.9%	4 2.0%	14 6.6%
Not in labor force	246 34.8%	161 37.5%	29 26.4%	53 30.7%	65 30.3%
Total	709 100.0%	429 100.0%	110 100.0%	172 100.0%	216 100.0%

TABLE 3.26 Industry of Current Job, by National Origin

Industry of Current Job	*Mexico*	*Cuba*	*Dominican Republic*	*Central America*	*South America*
Agriculture	73 12.3%	3 1.0%	6 6.6%	0 0.0%	0 0.0%
Construction	56 9.5%	9 2.7%	0 0.0%	7 4.7%	2 1.1%
Manufacturing	217 36.6%	99 29.8%	35 39.5%	39 27.5%	66 36.8%
Transportation/ communications	13 2.2%	21 6.4%	4 4.3%	18 12.7%	10 5.4%
Trade	61 10.3%	50 15.0%	18 20.6%	18 12.8%	42 23.8%
Finance	15 2.5%	15 4.6%	1 1.2%	7 5.3%	5 2.5%
Business	36 6.0%	36 11.0%	2 1.9%	4 3.1%	14 8.0%
Personal service	57 9.7%	28 8.4%	15 17.2%	20 13.9%	12 6.8%
Professional	55 9.2%	54 16.4%	7 8.3%	28 19.6%	21 12.0%
Other	9 1.6%	16 4.8%	0 0.4%	0 0.3%	6 3.6%
Total	592 100.0%	331 100.0%	90 100.0%	141 100.0%	178 100.0%

TABLE 3.27 Current Occupation, by National Origin

Current Occupation	*Mexico*	*Cuba*	*Dominican Republic*	*Central America*	*South America*
Household labor	18 3.1%	1 0.2%	7 7.0%	4 2.8%	6 3.2%
Service	70 11.8%	65 18.4%	17 18.0%	36 25.4%	26 14.4%
Farm labor	59 9.9%	1 0.2%	0 0.0%	0 0.0%	0 0.0%
Laborer	76 12.9%	21 6.0%	16 17.2%	4 3.0%	6 3.4%
Transport	21 3.5%	9 2.4%	1 1.2%	11 7.7%	12 6.6%
Operative	164 27.8%	57 16.2%	30 31.4%	29 20.3%	47 26.5%
Craftsperson	76 12.9%	59 16.7%	2 2.1%	13 9.0%	17 9.7%
Clerical	63 10.7%	49 14.0%	7 7.3%	15 10.4%	37 20.7%
Sales	5 0.8%	7 1.9%	5 5.0%	4 2.7%	4 2.5%
Manager	17 2.9%	31 9.0%	3 3.1%	7 4.7%	9 5.1%
Professional	21 3.6%	52 15.0%	7 7.7%	20 13.9%	14 7.9%
Total	589 100.0%	351 100.0%	95 100.0%	142 100.0%	178 100.0%

TABLE 3.28 Length of Service in Current Job, by National Origin

Length of Service for Current Employer (years)	*Mexico*	*Cuba*	*Dominican Republic*	*Central America*	*South America*
Five or fewer	248 48.7%	131 41.3%	58 63.2%	77 69.7%	78 52.1%
6-10	120 23.6%	101 32.0%	19 20.2%	20 18.4%	50 33.6%
11-20	106 20.9%	61 19.3%	15 16.6%	10 9.0%	19 12.9%
21 or more	34 6.7%	23 7.3%	0 0.0%	3 3.0%	2 1.5%
Total	508 100.0%	317 100.0%	92 100.0%	111 100.0%	150 100.0%

TABLE 3.29 Level of Job Satisfaction, by National Origin

Satisfaction with Current Job	*Mexico*	*Cuba*	*Dominican Republic*	*Central America*	*South America*
Very satisfied	370 58.1%	289 73.7%	57 53.6%	88 57.8%	105 53.6%
Somewhat satisfied	214 33.6%	87 22.1%	38 36.1%	52 34.1%	53 27.0%
Somewhat dissatisfied	43 6.7%	13 3.3%	6 6.1%	8 5.6%	23 11.6%
Very dissatisfied	10 1.6%	4 1.0%	5 4.3%	4 2.5%	15 7.8%
Total	637 100.0%	393 100.0%	106 100.0%	153 100.0%	196 100.0%

TABLE 3.30 Presently Working More than One Job, by National Origin

Currently Working More than One Job	*Mexico*	*Cuba*	*Dominican Republic*	*Central America*	*South America*
Yes	81 12.8%	73 18.5%	18 16.5%	20 12.8%	23 12.1%
No	551 87.2%	321 81.5%	89 83.5%	137 87.2%	171 87.9%
Total	632 100.0%	394 100.0%	106 100.0%	157 100.0%	195 100.0%

TABLE 3.31 Work Experience of Spouse (Among Married Respondents), by National Origin

Did Spouse Work for Pay in United States?	*Mexico*	*Cuba*	*Dominican Republic*	*Central America*	*South America*
Yes	450 87.2%	259 90.7%	60 83.6%	68 85.3%	119 85.0%
No	66 12.8%	27 9.3%	12 16.4%	12 14.7%	21 15.0%
Total	516 100.0%	286 100.0%	72 100.0%	80 100.0%	140 100.0%

TABLE 3.32 Spouse's Work Level, by National Origin

Work Level of Spouse's Current Job	*Mexico*	*Cuba*	*Dominican Republic*	*Central America*	*South America*
Full-time	288 64.2%	158 63.9%	45 74.9%	53 77.6%	89 75.5%
Part-time	41 9.1%	22 8.7%	6 9.7%	4 6.1%	13 10.7%
Not currently working	120 26.6%	68 27.4%	9 15.4%	11 16.4%	16 13.8%
Total	449 100.0%	247 100.0%	60 100.0%	68 100.0%	119 100.0%

TABLE 3.33 Industry of Spouse's Current Job, by National Origin

Industry of Spouse's Job	*Mexico*	*Cuba*	*Dominican Republic*	*Central America*	*South America*
Agriculture	56 13.5%	4 1.8%	0 0.0%	0 0.0%	0 0.5%
Construction	31 7.6%	24 9.6%	4 7.2%	3 4.6%	6 6.2%
Manufacturing	158 38.1%	79 32.1%	20 38.4%	17 27.2%	31 30.4%
Transportation/ communications	19 4.5%	29 11.9%	4 7.0%	7 11.1%	5 4.5%
Trade	52 12.6%	41 16.6%	12 23.3%	6 9.3%	22 21.5%
Finance	4 0.9%	9 3.7%	3 5.0%	2 2.5%	5 4.4%
Business	23 5.5%	18 7.3%	5 9.1%	6 9.4%	6 5.6%
Personal service	26 6.3%	19 7.5%	1 1.5%	10 15.6%	4 4.0%
Professional	36 8.6%	18 7.5%	3 6.5%	6 10.1%	14 13.4%
Other	10 2.4%	5 2.0%	1 2.1%	6 10.2%	10 9.5%
Total	414 100.0%	246 100.0%	52 100.0%	61 100.0%	103 100.0%

TABLE 3.34 Spouse's Current Occupation, by National Origin

Spouse's Current Occupation	*Mexico*	*Cuba*	*Dominican Republic*	*Central America*	*South America*
Household labor	12 2.8%	1 0.3%	0 0.0%	10 15.3%	0 0.3%
Service	56 13.0%	43 18.1%	11 20.7%	5 8.0%	18 16.2%
Farm labor	46 10.8%	2 0.7%	0 0.0%	0 0.0%	0 0.0%
Laborer	50 11.6%	12 5.1%	13 24.6%	3 5.1%	12 10.9%
Transport	11 2.5%	27 11.1%	1 2.1%	3 4.4%	5 4.0%
Operative	110 25.6%	50 21.1%	6 12.2%	11 18.0%	24 21.4%
Craftsperson	56 13.1%	48 20.1%	11 21.4%	10 16.5%	12 10.4%
Clerical	36 8.3%	18 7.4%	7 13.5%	8 12.0%	17 15.1%
Sales	4 0.9%	4 1.8%	0 0.0%	0 0.6%	1 0.7%
Manager	18 4.1%	19 8.1%	2 4.5%	5 8.5%	16 14.0%
Professional	31 7.2%	15 6.2%	1 1.1%	7 11.5%	8 6.9%
Total	429 100.0%	239 100.0%	52 100.0%	63 100.0%	113 100.0%

TABLE 3.35 Receipt of Assistance from Government Programs

Program	*Mexico*	*Cuba*	*Dominican Republic*	*Central America*	*South America*
Social Security	101 14.3% (n=706)	114 26.7% (n=426)	5 4.5% (n=110)	17 9.7% (n=171)	18 8.5% (n=216)
Medicare or Medicaid	85 12.0% (n=706)	96 22.5% (n=426)	29 26.2% (n=110)	30 17.3% (n=171)	16 7.2% (n=216)
Food stamps	73 10.3% (n=706)	31 7.3% (n=426)	23 21.2% (n=110)	10 5.8% (n=171)	8 3.7% (n=216)
Aid to Families With Dependent Children (AFDC)	18 2.5% (n=706)	10 2.4% (n=426)	9 8.0% (n=110)	7 3.9% (n=171)	8 3.7% (n=216)
Educational program assistance	12 1.7% (n=706)	5 1.1% (n=426)	4 4.0% (n=110)	13 7.4% (n=171)	20 9.2% (n=216)
Supplemental Security Income	21 2.9% (n=706)	10 2.3% (n=426)	5 4.3% (n=110)	13 7.4% (n=171)	1 0.3% (n=216)
Veterans program assistance	3 0.4% (n=706)	0 0.1% (n=426)	0 0.0% (n=110)	1 0.9% (n=171)	0 0.0% (n=216)
Housing program assistance	8 1.1% (n=706)	7 1.7% (n=426)	7 6.5% (n=110)	0 0.2% (n=171)	1 0.4% (n=216)
Other government programs	18 2.6% (n=706)	5 1.1% (n=426)	6 5.1% (n=110)	4 2.4% (n=171)	3 1.6% (n=216)

Note: This table combines several related questions. Because we asked the respondent about each of the programs listed above, we have included in each cell the number answering about each program from each national origin. We explain this style in greater depth in chapter two. Other tables following this alternative format are: 4.8, 4.9, 5.9, 5.10, 6.6, 6.11, 6.14, 6.39, 7.24, 7.25, 7.30, 7.31, 7.38, 7.40, 8.23, 8.24, 8.29, 8.30, 8.37, and 8.39.

TABLE 3.36 Tenancy, by National Origin

Tenancy	*Mexico*	*Cuba*	*Dominican Republic*	*Central America*	*South America*
Own	400 56.4%	268 62.8%	18 16.1%	59 34.4%	89 41.5%
Rent	289 40.9%	149 34.9%	91 82.4%	104 60.5%	116 53.9%
Other living arrangements	19 2.7%	10 2.3%	2 1.5%	9 5.1%	10 4.6%
Total	708 100.0%	427 100.0%	110 100.0%	172 100.0%	215 100.0%

TABLE 3.37 Year of Home Purchase, Among Homeowners, by National Origin

Period of Home Purchase	*Mexico*	*Cuba*	*Dominican Republic*	*Central America*	*South America*
1970 or before	66 17.2%	60 23.2%	1 4.5%	5 9.0%	2 2.6%
1971-1980	163 42.5%	90 34.8%	7 38.6%	19 31.8%	27 29.7%
1981-1988	155 40.3%	109 42.1%	10 56.9%	35 59.2%	61 67.7%
Total	385 100.0%	260 100.0%	18 100.0%	59 100.0%	89 100.0%

TABLE 3.38 Length of Residence in the Same Area, by National Origin

Residence in Same Area (years)	*Mexico*	*Cuba*	*Dominican Republic*	*Central America*	*South America*
5 or fewer	121 17.7%	99 23.5%	35 33.2%	64 39.1%	53 26.5%
6-10	188 27.5%	83 19.8%	41 39.0%	55 33.7%	78 38.7%
11-20	248 36.4%	150 35.8%	28 26.2%	26 15.9%	60 29.9%
21 or more	126 18.5%	88 20.9%	2 1.6%	19 11.3%	10 4.8%
Total	683 100.0%	419 100.0%	105 100.0%	164 100.0%	201 100.0%

Language Abilities

Findings

The majority of Latino immigrants, regardless of national origin, spoke Spanish at home (Table 3.39).

The rates of Spanish language use at home varied from 64 percent among Central Americans to 81 percent among Dominicans. Despite these high rates, significant numbers spoke either English predominantly or a mixture of English and Spanish.

Majorities of Central American and South American respondents reported that they spoke English either well or very well (Table 3.40). Approximately 30 percent of Dominican and Mexican respondents evaluated their English speaking ability in this manner. No more than 28 percent of any of the nationality groups reported that they could not speak English at all.

In general, respondents were more likely to report that they could *understand* English very well or well than they were to report that they could *speak* well or very well (Table 3.41). Majorities of the Cubans, Central Americans, and South Americans placed themselves in these categories as did 40 percent of Mexicans and 36 percent of Dominicans.

The levels reporting no English comprehension were lower than those reporting no English speaking ability. Almost no Central Americans or South Americans reported no English comprehension. Twenty percent of Dominicans, 13 percent of Mexicans, and 11 percent of Cubans reported no English comprehension.

Respondents were less likely to evaluate their English writing ability as well or very well than were they to report good English comprehension (Table 3.42). Slight majorities of Central Americans and South Americans reported that they could write English well or very well compared to 42 percent of Cubans, 29 percent of Mexicans, and 19 percent of Dominicans. Those reporting no writing ability ranged from 16 percent among South Americans to 42 percent among Mexicans.

Patterns of self-reported reading ability followed the patterns for writing ability (Table 3.43). The majority of Cubans as well as Central Americans and South Americans reported that they could read English either well or very well. Mexican and Dominican respondents were twice as likely as Cuban, Central American, or South American respondents to report that could not read English at all.

When we combined these four measures of self-reported English language skills (speaking, understanding, writing, and reading) into a single scale, we found that the majority of Central Americans and South Americans reported that they used English either well or very well (Table 3.44). Slightly less than a majority of Cubans (47 percent), 32 percent of Mexicans, and 21 percent of Dominicans assessed themselves in this manner.

Respondents reporting no English abilities across these four measures varied by national origin. At the low end were Central Americans and South Americans, with 6 and 5 percent respectively, reporting no English abilities. At the high end were Dominicans, nearly one-quarter of whom reported no English skills. In between were Cubans and Mexicans, at 16 and 19 percent, respectively.

We evaluated respondents' language abilities by asking them to interpret phrases from Spanish to English (Table 3.45). Among those respondents who tried to do so, most succeeded. Almost two-thirds of the Mexicans and Dominicans and half of the Cubans, however, did not attempt to interpret the phrases.

Regardless of national origin, the majority of Latino immigrants had taken English classes since immigrating (Table 3.46). Central Americans and South Americans showed the highest rates of English language class participation and Dominicans the lowest.

Again regardless of national origin, the majority of respondents reported that English is either important or very important to their jobs (Table 3.47). This evaluation of importance was particularly strong among Central Americans and South Americans.

Questions Asked: 29, 58, 62a, 62b, 62c, 62d, 63, and 64.
Tables with Comparable Data in Latino Voices: 2.28, 2.29, 4.9, and 10.24.

TABLE 3.39 Language Spoken at Home, by National Origin

Language Usually Spoken at Home	*Mexico*	*Cuba*	*Dominican Republic*	*Central America*	*South America*
English	66	48	5	19	24
	9.3%	11.1%	4.2%	11.1%	11.3%
Spanish	498	317	90	110	144
	70.2%	73.9%	81.1%	64.1%	66.8%
Both English and Spanish	146	64	16	43	47
	20.5%	15.0%	14.7%	24.8%	21.9%
Total	709	429	110	172	216
	100.0%	100.0%	100.0%	100.0%	100.0%

TABLE 3.40 Self-Evaluated English Speaking Ability, by National Origin

English Speaking Ability	*Mexico*	*Cuba*	*Dominican Republic*	*Central America*	*South America*
Very well	112 15.8%	124 28.9%	8 7.7%	41 23.9%	46 21.2%
Well	114 16.1%	76 17.7%	22 19.8%	52 30.1%	74 34.5%
Not well	315 44.4%	150 35.0%	50 45.0%	59 34.3%	69 32.0%
Not at all	168 23.7%	79 18.4%	30 27.5%	20 11.6%	27 12.3%
Total	709 100.0%	429 100.0%	110 100.0%	172 100.0%	216 100.0%

TABLE 3.41 Self-Evaluated English Listening Comprehension Ability, by National Origin

English Listening Comprehension Ability	*Mexico*	*Cuba*	*Dominican Republic*	*Central America*	*South America*
Very well	152 21.5%	142 33.1%	11 10.1%	79 45.8%	82 38.2%
Well	130 18.4%	92 21.5%	28 25.4%	43 24.8%	65 30.2%
Not well	333 47.0%	146 34.1%	49 44.6%	48 27.8%	66 30.5%
Not at all	93 13.2%	48 11.3%	22 19.9%	3 1.6%	2 1.1%
Total	709 100.0%	429 100.0%	110 100.0%	172 100.0%	216 100.0%

TABLE 3.42 Self-Evaluated English Writing Ability, by National Origin

English Writing Ability	*Mexico*	*Cuba*	*Dominican Republic*	*Central America*	*South America*
Very well	110 15.5%	125 29.2%	8 7.3%	63 36.6%	54 24.9%
Well	97 13.7%	56 13.0%	13 11.8%	26 15.3%	60 27.7%
Not well	207 29.2%	128 29.9%	45 40.6%	52 30.3%	67 31.3%
Not at all	295 41.6%	119 27.8%	45 40.3%	31 17.7%	35 16.1%
Total	709 100.0%	429 100.0%	110 100.0%	172 100.0%	216 100.0%

TABLE 3.43 Self-Evaluated English Reading Ability, by National Origin

English Reading Ability	*Mexico*	*Cuba*	*Dominican Republic*	*Central America*	*South America*
Very well	138 19.4%	141 32.9%	12 10.7%	55 32.2%	72 33.4%
Well	118 16.7%	84 19.6%	15 13.2%	38 22.0%	63 29.0%
Not well	251 35.4%	137 31.9%	49 44.4%	56 32.2%	55 25.6%
Not at all	202 28.5%	67 15.6%	35 31.7%	23 13.6%	26 12.0%
Total	708 100.0%	429 100.0%	110 100.0%	172 100.0%	216 100.0%

TABLE 3.44 Combined Self-Evaluated English Language Skills, by National Origin

Self-Evaluated English Language Skills	*Mexico*	*Cuba*	*Dominican Republic*	*Central America*	*South America*
Very well	109 15.3%	120 27.9%	8 7.7%	53 30.9%	52 23.9%
Well	117 16.5%	81 18.9%	15 13.7%	41 24.1%	72 33.5%
Mixed	34 4.8%	29 6.7%	9 8.1%	16 9.3%	13 6.0%
Not well	313 44.2%	133 31.0%	51 46.1%	51 29.9%	68 31.7%
Not at all	135 19.1%	66 15.5%	27 24.5%	10 5.9%	10 4.8%
Total	708 100.0%	429 100.0%	110 100.0%	172 100.0%	216 100.0%

TABLE 3.45 Interpretation Ability, by National Origin

Ability to Interpret Phrases from Spanish to English	*Mexico*	*Cuba*	*Dominican Republic*	*Central America*	*South America*
Did not attempt	440 62.6%	219 52.3%	72 65.2%	59 34.8%	78 39.1%
Tried and failed	15 2.1%	19 4.6%	9 8.0%	15 8.6%	8 4.0%
Tried and partially succeeded	23 3.2%	14 3.2%	4 3.7%	20 11.6%	7 3.6%
Succeeded	226 32.1%	167 39.9%	25 23.1%	76 45.0%	107 53.3%
Total	704 100.0%	420 100.0%	110 100.0%	170 100.0%	200 100.0%

TABLE 3.46 Study of English in the United States, by National Origin

Study of English Since Immigration	*Mexico*	*Cuba*	*Dominican Republic*	*Central America*	*South America*
Yes	439 61.9%	280 65.3%	62 55.8%	132 76.5%	163 75.5%
No	270 38.1%	149 34.7%	49 44.2%	40 23.5%	53 24.5%
Total	709 100.0%	429 100.0%	110 100.0%	172 100.0%	216 100.0%

TABLE 3.47 Importance of English to Job, by National Origin

Importance of Speaking English to Job	*Mexico*	*Cuba*	*Dominican Republic*	*Central America*	*South America*
Very important	277 43.4%	176 44.6%	41 38.4%	115 73.5%	129 66.1%
Somewhat important	150 23.5%	81 20.5%	20 19.1%	22 14.4%	32 16.3%
Not very important	124 19.5%	65 16.4%	28 26.1%	13 8.1%	27 13.9%
Not important	86 13.5%	73 18.5%	17 16.4%	6 4.0%	7 3.7%
Total	637 100.0%	394 100.0%	106 100.0%	156 100.0%	196 100.0%

Immigration and Citizenship Experiences

Findings

Mexican and Cuban immigration has been a long-standing component of twentieth-century migration to the United States. This pattern was evident among respondents to the National Latino Immigrant Survey. Approximately 17 percent of the Mexican and Cuban immigrants with at least five years of permanent residence immigrated prior to 1960 (Table 3.48). Few Dominicans, Central Americans, or South Americans immigrated prior to the 1960s and the majority came in the 1970s.

The majority of Dominican, Central American, and South American immigrants had fifteen or fewer years of U.S. residence (Table 3.49). The average length of residence for Mexican and Cuban immigrants was slightly longer, at sixteen to twenty years.

Mexicans tended to immigrate at younger ages than all other Latino immigrants (Table 3.50). Dominicans, Central Americans, and South Americans, on the other hand, were more likely than Mexicans to migrate as young adults. Cubans immigrated to the United States at all ages, with the largest share immigrating at age thirty-one and above.

Regardless of national origin, most Latino immigrants migrated with their families (Table 3.51). Cubans were the most likely and Dominicans the least likely to do so. More than 40 percent of Dominicans, Central Americans, and South Americans migrated alone.

Most Latino immigrants had networks of family and friends in place in the United States at the time of immigration (Table 3.52). The share of immigrants with neither family nor friends in the United States was quite low, ranging from 9 percent among Cuban immigrants to 24 percent among South American immigrants.

The majority of each of the Latino national origin groups had received their permanent residence visas ("green cards") since 1966 (Table 3.53). Only among Mexican and Cuban respondents were there sizable shares who had received visas prior to 1966. At the other extreme, 42 and 49 percent of South Americans and Central Americans, respectively, had received their green cards in the decade prior to the survey.

A narrow majority of all Latino national origin groups, with the exception of Dominicans, reported that they resided in the United States prior to receiving their permanent resident visas (Table 3.54). Central Americans were the most likely to have four or more years of residence prior to receiving their green cards. U.S. immigration law recognizes various immigrant statuses other than permanent residence. These include refugee visas, student visas, tourist visas, and short-term work visas. Another possibility is that some of these immigrants who had residence prior to immigration as permanent residents may have resided in the United States as undocumented immigrants prior to receiving their green cards.

More than three-quarters of the immigrants intended to make the United States their permanent homes at the time of immigration (Table 3.55). Between 8 percent (of Mexicans) and 18 percent (of South Americans) had no such intention.

The reasons for immigration varied by national origin (Table 3.56). Dominicans and Mexicans were most likely to report having migrated for economic reasons. By far, the most likely reason for Cuban migration was to flee communism. The reasons that Central Americans and South Americans migrated were less clear. Large components of the Central American population reported migrating for economic reasons, other reasons, and family reasons, with economic reasons being slightly more frequently mentioned. South American respondents divided their responses between economic reasons and other reasons.

The source of visa eligibility also varied among the Latino national origin groups (Table 3.57). More than 60 percent of Cubans obtained their visas based on their refugee status. Among Central Americans and South Americans, the most common source of permanent resident visa eligibility was job or professional status. Dominicans and Mexicans were more likely to attain visa eligibility through marriage to a U.S. citizen or as the child of a permanent resident.

The majority of Latino immigrants migrated from urban areas (Table 3.58). Mexicans and Dominicans were the most likely to have rural origins.

On average, Latino immigrants, with the exception of Cubans, had visited their home countries, but made less than one visit per year of residence (Table 3.59). More than three-quarters of Cuban immigrants, on the other hand, had not returned to Cuba since they immigrated. Dominicans were more likely than any of the other Latino national origin groups to have returned to the country of origin since immigration.

With the exception of Cuban immigrants, the majority of Latino immigrants had not naturalized (Table 3.60). Mexican immigrants showed the lowest rates of naturalization.

Among the naturalized, between 71 and 78 percent became U.S. citizens as the result of their own naturalization (Table 3.61). The remainder became U.S. citizens when their parents naturalized. The INS characterizes this process as "derivative citizenship" in which the parent, upon naturalization, files a form to include his or her minor children as U.S. citizens. The rates of derivative citizenship were relatively constant across national origin groups.

Narrow majorities of Mexican, Dominican, Central American, and South American households were comprised exclusively of non-U.S. citizen adults (Table 3.62). Interestingly, the household milieu of many non-U.S. citizens included U.S. citizen adults.

These permanent resident households also included a small number of non-U.S. citizens without permanent residence (Table 3.63). Between 19 and 43 percent of Latino immigrant households did not report on the U.S. residence status of non-citizen household adults.

Overwhelming majorities of each of the Latino national origin groups continued to have close relatives residing in the country of origin (Table 3.64). These levels of close family members in the home country exceeded 90 percent for all nationalities but Cubans.

Most respondents had close relatives in the United States who did not live in the household (Table 3.65). South Americans were the least likely to have relatives in the United States.

Questions Asked: K, L, M, 2, 3, 4, 5, 6, 7, 8, 9, 12, 13, 14, 16, 67, 69, and 76.
Tables with Comparable Data in Latino Voices: 2.32, 2.34, 10.16, and 10.19.

TABLE 3.48 Decade of Immigration, by National Origin

Decade of Immigration to Permanent Residence	*Mexico*	*Cuba*	*Dominican Republic*	*Central America*	*South America*
1950s or before	112 16.7%	70 17.9%	1 1.5%	9 5.8%	10 5.8%
1960s	198 29.5%	196 50.1%	37 37.1%	45 29.6%	49 27.3%
1970s	303 45.2%	119 30.4%	56 55.2%	77 50.5%	105 58.2%
1980s	57 8.5%	6 1.6%	6 6.3%	21 14.1%	15 8.6%
Total	671 100.0%	391 100.0%	101 100.0%	152 100.0%	180 100.0%

TABLE 3.49 Length of U.S. Residence, by National Origin

Length of U.S. Residence (years)	*Mexico*	*Cuba*	*Dominican Republic*	*Central America*	*South America*
10 or fewer	150 22.3%	78 20.0%	34 34.1%	58 38.3%	56 31.2%
11-15	140 20.8%	23 6.0%	22 21.8%	36 23.7%	42 23.6%
16-20	167 24.8%	106 27.1%	23 22.4%	20 13.5%	43 24.1%
21-30	124 18.5%	147 37.5%	22 21.8%	31 20.3%	31 17.1%
31 or more	91 13.5%	37 9.4%	0 0.0%	6 4.2%	7 4.0%
Total	671 100.0%	391 100.0%	101 100.0%	152 100.0%	180 100.0%

TABLE 3.50 Age at Immigration, by National Origin

Age at Immigration	*Mexico*	*Cuba*	*Dominican Republic*	*Central America*	*South America*
6 or younger	67 9.6%	52 12.4%	6 5.3%	7 3.8%	8 3.7%
7-18	262 37.4%	80 18.9%	23 20.5%	51 29.6%	56 25.8%
19-30	260 37.2%	106 25.0%	52 47.4%	75 43.9%	112 52.0%
31 or older	111 15.8%	186 43.8%	29 26.7%	39 22.7%	40 18.6%
Total	699 100.0%	424 100.0%	110 100.0%	171 100.0%	216 100.0%

TABLE 3.51 Who Accompanied Respondents to the United States at the Time of Immigration, by National Origin

Who Accompanied Respondent Upon Immigration?	*Mexico*	*Cuba*	*Dominican Republic*	*Central America*	*South America*
Family	468 66.0%	343 80.0%	55 50.0%	92 53.2%	118 54.9%
Friends	25 3.6%	3 0.6%	7 6.1%	7 4.2%	4 1.9%
Family and friends	20 2.9%	14 3.2%	1 1.1%	1 0.6%	7 3.1%
Immigrated alone	196 27.6%	70 16.2%	47 42.8%	72 41.9%	86 40.1%
Total	709 100.0%	429 100.0%	110 100.0%	172 100.0%	216 100.0%

TABLE 3.52 People Who Lived in the United States When Respondent Immigrated, by National Origin

Who Lived in the U.S. at the Time of Immigration?	*Mexico*	*Cuba*	*Dominican Republic*	*Central America*	*South America*
Family	389 55.1%	183 42.8%	68 61.7%	100 58.4%	106 51.0%
Friends	43 6.1%	44 10.2%	3 2.7%	19 10.8%	28 13.5%
Family and friends	152 21.6%	164 38.2%	28 25.6%	30 17.3%	25 12.0%
No one	122 17.2%	38 8.8%	11 10.0%	23 13.6%	49 23.5%
Total	707 100.0%	429 100.0%	110 100.0%	172 100.0%	207 100.0%

TABLE 3.53 Year Received Permanent Resident (Legal Immigrant) Visa, by National Origin

Year Received Permanent Resident Visa	*Mexico*	*Cuba*	*Dominican Republic*	*Central America*	*South America*
1965 or before	174 25.9%	133 33.7%	15 13.9%	23 13.6%	17 8.0%
1966-1978	304 45.1%	165 41.7%	74 68.9%	65 37.9%	107 49.9%
1979-1988	195 29.0%	97 24.7%	19 17.3%	84 48.5%	90 42.1%
Total	673 100.0%	395 100.0%	107 100.0%	172 100.0%	214 100.0%

TABLE 3.54 Years of Residence in the United States Before Receiving Permanent Resident Visa, by National Origin

Years of Residence Prior to Receiving Immigrant Visa	*Mexico*	*Cuba*	*Dominican Republic*	*Central America*	*South America*
None	347 49.0%	163 37.9%	62 55.7%	71 41.2%	100 46.4%
1-3	106 15.0%	117 27.3%	25 22.7%	26 15.1%	55 25.4%
4-10	186 26.3%	137 32.0%	19 17.0%	58 33.4%	49 22.6%
More than 10	69 9.7%	12 2.8%	5 4.6%	18 10.2%	12 5.6%
Total	709 100.0%	429 100.0%	110 100.0%	172 100.0%	216 100.0%

TABLE 3.55 Respondent's Intention to Make the United States the Permanent Home at the Time of Immigration, by National Origin

Plans to Make the United States the Permanent Home at Immigration	*Mexico*	*Cuba*	*Dominican Republic*	*Central America*	*South America*
Yes	599 85.3%	369 86.4%	91 85.1%	132 76.8%	167 77.5%
No	54 7.8%	44 10.3%	15 13.5%	28 16.3%	40 18.4%
Was not sure	49 6.9%	14 3.3%	1 1.4%	12 7.0%	9 4.1%
Total	702 100.0%	427 100.0%	107 100.0%	172 100.0%	216 100.0%

TABLE 3.56 Reason for Immigration, by National Origin

Reason for Immigration	*Mexico*	*Cuba*	*Dominican Republic*	*Central America*	*South America*
Join family	200 28.5%	40 9.3%	31 27.9%	45 25.9%	38 17.7%
Flee political strife	1 0.2%	81 19.0%	3 2.7%	13 7.6%	2 0.8%
Flee communism	0 0.0%	213 49.9%	0 0.0%	4 2.2%	0 0.0%
Economic reasons	301 42.9%	37 8.8%	59 53.1%	57 33.2%	85 39.5%
Accompany family	76 10.8%	11 2.6%	4 3.4%	6 3.4%	15 7.0%
Other	123 17.6%	45 10.5%	14 12.8%	48 27.8%	75 35.0%
Total	702 100.0%	427 100.0%	110 100.0%	172 100.0%	214 100.0%

TABLE 3.57 Reason for Visa Eligibility, by National Origin

Reason for Visa Eligibility	*Mexico*	*Cuba*	*Dominican Republic*	*Central America*	*South America*
Refugee	13 1.8%	258 60.2%	0 0.0%	20 11.8%	7 3.3%
Parent of a U.S. citizen	66 9.3%	7 1.6%	19 17.1%	12 6.7%	20 9.3%
Child of a U.S. citizen	75 10.6%	11 2.5%	2 2.2%	14 7.9%	5 2.2%
Sibling of a U.S. citizen	34 4.8%	16 3.7%	6 5.1%	6 3.6%	27 12.5%
Spouse of a U.S. citizen	176 24.8%	8 1.8%	28 25.7%	23 13.2%	39 18.2%
Child of a resident alien	157 22.2%	54 12.6%	27 24.5%	31 17.7%	29 13.4%
Job or professional skills	130 18.3%	28 6.5%	18 16.2%	42 24.2%	68 31.5%
Other	58 8.2%	48 11.2%	10 9.3%	25 14.8%	20 9.5%
Total	709 100.0%	429 100.0%	110 100.0%	172 100.0%	216 100.0%

TABLE 3.58 Rural or Urban Residence in Country of Origin, by National Origin

Rural or Urban Area of Origin	*Mexico*	*Cuba*	*Dominican Republic*	*Central America*	*South America*
Rural	319 45.2%	67 15.6%	41 36.8%	25 14.3%	17 8.0%
Urban	386 54.8%	360 84.4%	70 63.2%	147 85.7%	198 92.0%
Total	705 100.0%	426 100.0%	110 100.0%	172 100.0%	216 100.0%

TABLE 3.59 Number of Visits to Home Country Per Year, by National Origin

Visits to Home Country Per Year of Residence	*Mexico*	*Cuba*	*Dominican Republic*	*Central America*	*South America*
No visits	169 24.9%	329 77.9%	9 9.2%	68 42.0%	51 27.5%
One visit per year or less	357 52.8%	90 21.2%	84 83.0%	88 54.4%	126 68.5%
More than one and less than three visits per year	65 9.5%	1 0.2%	8 7.8%	6 3.6%	5 2.9%
Three or more visits per year	86 12.7%	3 0.7%	0 0.0%	0 0.0%	2 1.1%
Total	677 100.0%	423 100.0%	101 100.0%	163 100.0%	183 100.0%

TABLE 3.60 Citizenship Status of Respondents, by National Origin

Citizenship Status	*Mexico*	*Cuba*	*Dominican Republic*	*Central America*	*South America*
U.S. citizen	159 22.5%	232 54.2%	33 29.8%	62 36.1%	64 29.9%
Permanent resident	550 77.5%	196 45.8%	78 70.2%	110 63.9%	151 70.1%
Total	709 100.0%	429 100.0%	110 100.0%	172 100.0%	216 100.0%

TABLE 3.61 Type of Naturalization, by National Origin

Source of Naturalization	*Mexico*	*Cuba*	*Dominican Republic*	*Central America*	*South America*
Own naturalization	112 70.8%	175 76.2%	21 74.2%	48 70.4%	52 77.9%
Naturalization of parents or "derivative" citizens	46 29.2%	55 23.8%	7 25.8%	20 29.6%	15 22.1%
Total	159 100.0%	230 100.0%	29 100.0%	68 100.0%	67 100.0%

TABLE 3.62 Citizenship Status of Adults in Household, by National Origin

Citizenship Status of Adults in the Household	*Mexico*	*Cuba*	*Dominican Republic*	*Central America*	*South America*
All non-U.S. citizens	342 50.3%	120 30.7%	60 59.0%	77 51.1%	110 55.6%
Mixed U.S and non-U.S. citizens	208 30.6%	94 23.9%	13 12.7%	24 15.9%	35 17.9%
All U.S. citizens	130 19.0%	178 45.4%	29 28.3%	49 33.0%	52 26.5%
Total	680 100.0%	392 100.0%	102 100.0%	150 100.0%	198 100.0%

TABLE 3.63 Resident Status of Adults in the Household, by National Origin

Resident Status of Household Adults	*Mexico*	*Cuba*	*Dominican Republic*	*Central America*	*South America*
All permanent residents or citizens	551 77.7%	239 55.7%	80 72.3%	115 66.6%	148 68.6%
Some non-permanent residents	26 3.6%	6 1.3%	0 0.0%	6 3.4%	5 2.5%
Did not report	133 18.7%	185 43.0%	31 27.7%	52 29.9%	62 28.9%
Total	709 100.0%	429 100.0%	110 100.0%	172 100.0%	216 100.0%

TABLE 3.64 Close Relatives Living in Home Country, by National Origin

Close Relatives Living in Home Country	*Mexico*	*Cuba*	*Dominican Republic*	*Central America*	*South America*
Yes	660 93.3%	342 79.7%	109 98.5%	162 94.1%	201 93.5%
No	48 6.7%	87 20.3%	2 1.5%	10 5.9%	14 6.5%
Total	708 100.0%	429 100.0%	110 100.0%	172 100.0%	216 100.0%

TABLE 3.65 Close Relatives Living in the United States, but Outside Household, by National Origin

Close Relatives Living in the United States, but Outside Household	*Mexico*	*Cuba*	*Dominican Republic*	*Central America*	*South America*
Yes	612 86.5%	385 89.7%	102 92.5%	144 84.1%	156 72.4%
No	95 13.5%	44 10.3%	8 7.5%	27 15.9%	60 27.6%
Total	708 100.0%	429 100.0%	110 100.0%	172 100.0%	216 100.0%

4

Nationality, Ethnic, Associational, and Linguistic Characteristics of Latino Immigrants

The focus of this chapter is the degree to which Latino immigrants feel connected to different aspects of U.S. society. We examine the peer, family, and workplace environments of Latino immigrants to determine the levels of U.S. citizenship among these associates and their race or national origin. We look at the organizational behavior of Latino immigrants and, then, the ethnicity of the membership of the organizations to which Latino immigrants belong. Finally, we look at the language used to obtain information through the media. Each of these measures indicates that Latino immigrants are acculturating and integrating into American society. Latino immigrants associate with U.S. citizens, their associational networks include non-Latinos as well as Latinos, and many are members of community organizations, some of which have non-Latino majorities. Finally, many immigrants, and in some cases most, receive media information in English. Needless to say, these generalizations apply at different rates to each of the Latino national origin groups.

Nationality Characteristics of Associates

Findings

At the time of immigration, Mexican, Cuban, and South American immigrants entered social networks in which more friends were U.S. citizens than were non-citizens (Table 4.1). Dominican and Central American immigrants had more peers who were non-citizens than were citizens. Most respondents were aware of the citizenship status of their peers.

At the time of the survey, solid majorities of the relatives of each of the nationality groups were U.S. citizens (Table 4.2). Cubans were the most likely to report that their relatives were U.S. citizens.

Among respondents with parents who resided in the United States, few had parents who naturalized (Table 4.3). Cuban respondents were the most likely to report that one or both parents naturalized.

Few respondents reported that none of their peers at the time of the survey was a U.S. citizen (Table 4.4). Ranging from a low of 2 percent with no U.S.-citizen peers among Cubans and Dominicans to a high of 16 percent for Central Americans, these findings indicate that most Latino immigrants associate with citizens as well as with non-citizens. At the other extreme, more than half of Cuban respondents reported that most of their friends were U.S. citizens.

Questions Asked: 5a, 17, 18, and 45.
Tables with Comparable Data in Latino Voices: None.

TABLE 4.1 Citizenship Status of Peers at Time of Immigration, by National Origin

Citizenship Status of Peers at Time of Immigration	*Mexico*	*Cuba*	*Dominican Republic*	*Central America*	*South America*
U.S. citizens	97 49.5%	92 47.7%	10 31.2%	16 32.9%	24 46.1%
Non-U.S. citizens	90 46.2%	55 28.4%	16 51.4%	32 67.1%	21 39.6%
Not sure	8 4.3%	46 23.8%	5 17.5%	0 0.0%	7 14.3%
Total	195 100.0%	192 100.0%	31 100.0%	48 100.0%	52 100.0%

TABLE 4.2 Citizenship Status of Relatives, by National Origin

Citizenship Status of Relatives	*Mexico*	*Cuba*	*Dominican Republic*	*Central America*	*South America*
U.S. citizens	415 69.7%	326 85.4%	67 65.6%	105 73.8%	99 64.2%
Non-U.S. citizens	181 30.3%	56 14.6%	35 34.4%	37 26.2%	55 35.8%
Total	595 100.0%	382 100.0%	102 100.0%	142 100.0%	153 100.0%

TABLE 4.3 Citizenship Status of Parents, by National Origin

Parents' Naturalization Status	*Mexico*	*Cuba*	*Dominican Republic*	*Central America*	*South America*
Parents did not live in the United States	244 34.8%	116 27.5%	39 36.0%	50 28.9%	108 50.7%
Both became U.S. citizens	46 6.5%	73 17.4%	5 4.3%	23 13.4%	8 3.7%
Father became U.S. citizen	49 7.0%	26 6.1%	12 10.5%	3 2.0%	1 0.6%
Mother became U.S. citizen	45 6.5%	9 2.1%	7 6.1%	6 3.2%	6 3.0%
Neither became U.S. citizen	318 45.3%	198 46.9%	47 43.2%	90 52.4%	89 42.0%
Total	703 100.0%	422 100.0%	110 100.0%	172 100.0%	213 100.0%

TABLE 4.4 Citizenship Status of Peers, by National Origin

Citizenship Status of Peers	*Mexico*	*Cuba*	*Dominican Republic*	*Central America*	*South America*
Most are U.S. citizens	219 34.1%	257 63.5%	31 34.5%	37 23.4%	71 37.3%
Some are U.S. citizens	228 35.5%	107 26.3%	35 38.4%	51 32.2%	63 33.2%
Few are U.S. citizens	137 21.2%	34 8.4%	23 25.2%	45 28.9%	47 24.4%
None are U.S. citizens	59 9.2%	7 1.7%	2 1.9%	24 15.5%	10 5.1%
Total	643 100.0%	404 100.0%	90 100.0%	157 100.0%	191 100.0%

Racial and Ethnic Milieu of Latino Immigrants

Findings

Latinos constituted the bulk of the co-workers of a majority of Mexican and Cuban immigrants (Table 4.5), but just a plurality of the co-workers of other Latino nationality groups. More than 20 percent of the Dominican and South American respondents reported that their co-workers were best described as multi-ethnic.

The majority of Mexican, Cuban, and Dominican immigrants resided in neighborhoods with other Latinos (Table 4.6). Dominicans were the most likely to report that they lived around other Latinos. Central Americans and South Americans, on the other hand, were about equally likely to report residing around Latinos or whites, with those reporting Latino neighbors slightly more prevalent.

The majority of Latino immigrants neither associated exclusively with Latinos nor with non-Latinos (Table 4.7). Mexican immigrants were the most likely to report that their peers were exclusively Latino. South Americans were the most likely to report that some or none of their friends were Latino.

Questions Asked: 28, 43, and 44.
Tables with Comparable Data in Latino Voices: 4.12.

TABLE 4.5 Race/Ethnicity of Co-Workers, by National Origin

Race/Ethnicity of Most of Co-Workers	*Mexico*	*Cuba*	*Dominican Republic*	*Central America*	*South America*
Latinos	440 69.3%	233 61.0%	53 49.6%	73 47.1%	71 36.5%
(Non-Latino) Whites	105 16.6%	75 19.6%	26 24.5%	46 29.5%	58 30.0%
Blacks	9 1.4%	5 1.4%	3 3.0%	1 0.7%	12 6.0%
Asians	8 1.3%	20 5.3%	0 0.0%	3 2.2%	0 0.2%
A mix of races/ethnicities	53 8.3%	38 9.9%	22 20.2%	27 17.7%	48 24.8%
Work alone or in family business	20 3.1%	11 2.8%	3 2.7%	5 2.9%	5 2.5%
Total	634 100.0%	382 100.0%	107 100.0%	155 100.0%	194 100.0%

TABLE 4.6 Race/Ethnicity of Respondent's Neighborhood, by National Origin

Race/Ethnicity of People in Neighborhood	*Mexico*	*Cuba*	*Dominican Republic*	*Central America*	*South America*
Latinos	447 63.6%	252 59.3%	82 75.3%	59 34.5%	83 39.3%
(Non-Latino) Whites	170 24.1%	117 27.7%	11 9.8%	57 33.4%	77 36.2%
Blacks	16 2.2%	10 2.4%	6 5.4%	21 12.3%	7 3.4%
Asians	8 1.2%	17 3.9%	0 0.0%	8 4.6%	3 1.5%
A mixture of races/ethnicities	62 8.8%	29 6.8%	10 9.6%	26 15.1%	42 19.6%
Total	704 100.0%	425 100.0%	109 100.0%	171 100.0%	212 100.0%

TABLE 4.7 Latino Peers, by National Origin

Share of Latinos Among Peers	*Mexico*	*Cuba*	*Dominican Republic*	*Central America*	*South America*
All	253 36.2%	132 31.1%	36 32.5%	44 26.0%	55 25.9%
Most	308 44.2%	212 49.9%	57 52.3%	62 36.7%	60 28.1%
Some	120 17.2%	74 17.4%	11 10.4%	56 33.1%	91 42.8%
None	17 2.4%	7 1.6%	5 4.8%	7 4.2%	7 3.2%
Total	698 100.0%	424 100.0%	110 100.0%	169 100.0%	212 100.0%

Organizational Activity of Latino Immigrants

Findings

The majority of all Latino national origin groups, with the exception of South Americans, reported that they were members of churches (Table 4.8). Central Americans were the most likely to report church membership. No other community organization saw such high rates of Latino immigrant membership. Parent Teacher Associations (PTA) were the next most frequently mentioned organization.

Few Latino immigrants were members of unions, senior citizen clubs, political organizations, or national-origin clubs.

Among Latinos who were members of churches, the majority reported that most other members were Latino (Table 4.9). Latino union members, with the exception of the few Dominicans who were union members, were members of unions with non-Latino majorities.

The national origin of the members of PTAs to which Latinos belonged varied. Mexicans and Dominicans reported that Latinos made up the majority of PTAs to which they belonged. Central Americans and South Americans, on the other hand, were likely to report that most of the members of PTAs to which they belonged were not Latino.

Questions Asked: 48 and 48a.
Tables with Comparable Data in Latino Voices: 2.26, 3.21, and 8.2.

TABLE 4.8 Membership in Community Organizations, by National Origin

Type of Organization	*Mexico*	*Cuba*	*Dominican Republic*	*Central America*	*South America*
Church	422 59.6% (n=709)	284 66.1% (n=429)	75 67.7% (n=110)	121 70.3% (n=172)	97 44.9% (n=216)
PTA	190 26.9% (n=709)	91 21.3% (n=429)	23 20.8% (n=110)	36 21.0% (n=172)	47 21.9% (n=216)
Sports club	98 13.8% (n=709)	46 10.8% (n=429)	10 9.3% (n=110)	32 18.5% (n=172)	43 19.8% (n=216)
Social club	74 10.4% (n=709)	44 10.2% (n=429)	8 7.4% (n=110)	20 11.7% (n=172)	39 18.2% (n=216)
National-origin club	62 8.8% (n=709)	39 9.1% (n=429)	9 8.2% (n=110)	25 14.5% (n=172)	27 12.7% (n=216)
Union	68 9.7% (n=709)	42 9.8% (n=429)	9 7.9% (n=110)	26 15.6% (n=168)	8 3.6% (n=216)
Political club	17 2.3% (n=709)	28 6.5% (n=429)	0 0.0% (n=110)	10 6.1% (n=172)	5 2.4% (n=216)
Fraternal club	10 1.3% (n=709)	24 5.6% (n=429)	6 5.7% (n=110)	3 1.9% (n=172)	23 10.7% (n=216)
Senior citizens club	14 1.9% (n=708)	16 3.8% (n=429)	5 4.2% (n=110)	2 1.2% (n=172)	1 0.4% (n=216)

TABLE 4.9 Latinos in Organizations to Which the Respondent Belonged, by National Origin

Type of Organization	Mexico	Cuba	Dominican Republic	Central America	South America
Majority Latino church	361 86.2% (n=419)	221 78.0% (n=283)	58 77.2% (n=75)	88 72.4% (n=121)	55 58.1% (n=95)
Majority Latino PTA	108 57.2% (n=189)	44 49.0% (n=90)	12 50.5% (n=23)	10 28.5% (n=36)	7 14.1% (n=47)
Majority Latino sports club	67 69.5% (n=96)	20 44.4% (n=45)	7 67.6% (n=10)	23 73.4% (n=32)	13 30.7% (n=43)
Majority Latino social club	57 76.8% (n=74)	29 66.8% (n=44)	5 59.3% (n=8)	8 40.3% (n=19)	20 51.6% (n=39)
Majority Latino nationality club	60 95.9% (n=62)	39 99.0% (n=39)	9 100.0% (n=9)	24 97.3% (n=25)	27 100.0% (n=27)
Majority Latino union	29 44.2% (n=67)	15 35.5% (n=41)	5 52.7% (n=9)	5 20.5% (n=26)	2 26.2% (n=7)
Majority Latino political club	13 78.1% (n=17)	25 90.4% (n=28)	0 0.0% (n=0)	1 5.8% (n=9)	1 20.2% (n=5)
Majority Latino fraternal club	8 95.3% (n=8)	17 76.7% (n=22)	5 80.9% (n=6)	1 28.2% (n=3)	7 30.8% (n=23)
Majority Latino seniors club	4 29.6% (n=14)	10 63.5% (n=15)	5 100.0% (n=5)	1 63.1% (n=2)	1 100.0% (n=1)

Linguistic Patterns of Latino Immigrants

Findings

The language of newspapers read varied by national origin (Table 4.10). Among Mexicans, Central Americans, and South Americans who read newspapers, more reported reading papers in English than in Spanish. Cubans and Dominicans were more likely to report reading papers in Spanish.

Few Latino immigrants reported that they did not read a newspaper. Dominicans were the most likely not to read a newspaper and South Americans the least likely.

Language of radio stations listened to also varied by national origin (Table 4.11). Mexicans, Cubans, and Dominicans were more likely to listen to Spanish-language radio while Central Americans and South Americans were more likely to rely on English radio.

Between 20 and 40 percent of respondents reported that they listened to radio in both Spanish and English. These rates of bilingual radio listenership were higher than those for bilingual newspaper readership.

With the exception of Dominicans, the majority of each of the Latino national-origin groups watched more English-language television than Spanish television (Table 4.12). Among Dominicans, equal numbers watched English and Spanish television. Few Latinos did not watch television at all.

The majority of each national origin group, except for Dominicans, owned a video cassette recorder (VCR) (Table 4.13). More than most other data reported here, these may reflect the period of the interview. In the years since 1988 when these data were collected, VCR ownership has become even more pervasive.

Questions Asked: 59, 60, 61, and 104.
Tables with Comparable Data in Latino Voices: 5.2.

TABLE 4.10 Language of Newspapers Read, by National Origin

Language of Newspapers Read	*Mexico*	*Cuba*	*Dominican Republic*	*Central America*	*South America*
English	279 39.4%	124 28.9%	19 17.5%	87 50.5%	118 54.9%
Spanish	264 37.3%	174 40.8%	61 55.0%	44 25.6%	48 22.2%
Both languages	101 14.3%	102 24.0%	15 13.4%	36 21.2%	46 21.5%
Do not read newspapers	64 9.1%	27 6.3%	16 14.1%	5 2.7%	3 1.5%
Total	709 100.0%	428 100.0%	110 100.0%	172 100.0%	216 100.0%

TABLE 4.11 Language of Radio Stations Listened To, by National Origin

Language of Radio Stations Listened To	*Mexico*	*Cuba*	*Dominican Republic*	*Central America*	*South America*
English	178 25.1%	131 30.6%	13 11.6%	75 43.4%	91 42.7%
Spanish	335 47.3%	188 43.9%	51 46.0%	42 24.3%	55 25.7%
Both languages	188 26.5%	90 20.9%	44 39.5%	54 31.4%	58 27.2%
Do not listen to radio	8 1.2%	20 4.6%	3 2.9%	2 0.9%	9 4.4%
Total	709 100.0%	429 100.0%	110 100.0%	172 100.0%	214 100.0%

TABLE 4.12 Language of Television Stations Watched, by National Origin

Language of Television Stations Watched	*Mexico*	*Cuba*	*Dominican Republic*	*Central America*	*South America*
English	266 37.5%	163 37.9%	32 29.3%	94 54.3%	120 55.8%
Spanish	210 29.7%	119 27.7%	32 29.3%	17 10.1%	24 11.3%
Both languages	226 31.8%	146 34.0%	43 38.5%	60 35.0%	68 31.7%
Do not watch television	7 1.0%	2 0.4%	3 2.8%	1 0.5%	3 1.2%
Total	709 100.0%	429 100.0%	110 100.0%	172 100.0%	216 100.0%

TABLE 4.13 Video Cassette Recorder Ownership, by National Origin

VCR Ownership	*Mexico*	*Cuba*	*Dominican Republic*	*Central America*	*South America*
Yes	460 64.9%	306 71.5%	48 43.5%	125 72.5%	140 65.3%
No	249 35.1%	122 28.5%	62 56.5%	47 27.5%	75 34.7%
Total	709 100.0%	428 100.0%	110 100.0%	172 100.0%	215 100.0%

5

Latino Immigrant Political Access, Values, and Participation

Despite the fact that approximately two-thirds of Latino immigrants eligible for U.S. citizenship had not yet naturalized, they did report being engaged in U.S. politics. This evidence of engagement came despite a perception among a majority of Latino immigrants that U.S. society and, to a lesser degree, the Immigration and Naturalization Service, discriminated against Latinos. The engagement took several forms. Latino immigrants reported participating in various forms of political activity, particularly following politics in the news. Among the naturalized, a high percentage was registered to vote.

The fact that Latinos who are naturalized are engaged and interested in politics reveals the political potential that Latinos might have if more were naturalized. Not only did the naturalized have high voter registration rates—higher on average than the population as a whole—their voter turnout rates were also quite high. Latino immigrants followed the pattern of the population as a whole, turning out in lower numbers for local and school board elections than for state and national races. Of particular note in these data are the rates for Mexican-origin U.S. citizens. In state and local elections, they showed the highest rates of voter turnout. In sum, these indicators of political interest and political activity among Latinos demonstrate just how meaningful a Latino electoral empowerment strategy based on mass naturalization could be. In the next chapter, we examine levels of interest in naturalization and the procedural impediments faced by Latinos who want to become United States citizens.

Perceptions of Discrimination

With the exception of Cubans, the majority of each of the Latino national origin groups perceived that U.S. society discriminates against

Latinos (Table 5.1). Central Americans were the most likely to perceive this.

Despite the general perception among all but Cuban immigrants of societal discrimination, few reported that they or their families had experienced discrimination (Table 5.2). South Americans were the most likely to report having been the target of discrimination; slightly more than one-quarter reported this experience. Dominicans were the least likely to report discrimination, with slightly more than 10 percent having experienced it.

Among those who experienced discrimination, the frequencies varied by national origin (Table 5.3). More than two-thirds of Cubans and Dominicans who had encountered discrimination reported that this experience was rare. Mexicans were also more likely than other Latino immigrants to report that their experience with discrimination was rare. Central Americans and South Americans were more likely to report that their or their families' experiences with discrimination were occasional rather than rare or frequent.

Few respondents reported that they or their families experienced frequent discrimination. Just 3 percent of Dominicans who had experienced discrimination reported that their experience was frequent. At the other extreme, nearly 30 percent of South Americans reported experiencing frequent discrimination.

Fewer respondents reported that INS discriminated against Latinos than reported that U.S. society as a whole discriminated (Table 5.4). Many, however, were not sure if INS discriminated. Approximately one-quarter of Mexicans, Cubans, Central Americans, and South Americans and 40 percent of Dominicans reported that they were not sure if INS discriminated. INS scored much higher rates of doubt than did the society as a whole (Table 5.1).

Questions Asked: 54, 55, 56, and 100.
Tables with Comparable Data in Latino Voices: 7.5, 7.10, 7.11, 7.12, 10.41, 10.46, 10.47, and 10.48.

TABLE 5.1 Perception of Discrimination Against Latinos, by National Origin

Does U.S. Society Discriminate Against Latinos?	*Mexico*	*Cuba*	*Dominican Republic*	*Central America*	*South America*
Yes	352 52.6%	170 42.5%	61 56.1%	119 71.1%	120 60.3%
No	289 43.2%	222 55.6%	42 38.5%	44 26.3%	76 38.4%
Unsure	28 4.3%	8 1.9%	6 5.5%	4 2.6%	3 1.3%
Total	670 100.0%	399 100.0%	109 100.0%	168 100.0%	199 100.0%

TABLE 5.2 Personal or Familial Experience of Discrimination, by National Origin

Has Respondent's Family Experienced Discrimination?	*Mexico*	*Cuba*	*Dominican Republic*	*Central America*	*South America*
Yes	152 21.7%	74 17.2%	12 11.2%	37 21.6%	59 27.5%
No	550 78.3%	354 82.8%	97 88.8%	134 78.4%	155 72.5%
Total	703 100.0%	428 100.0%	109 100.0%	171 100.0%	214 100.0%

TABLE 5.3 Frequency of Familial Discrimination, by National Origin

Frequency of Familial Discrimination	*Mexico*	*Cuba*	*Dominican Republic*	*Central America*	*South America*
Rarely	75 49.5%	48 68.7%	9 74.3%	13 34.4%	18 33.7%
Occasionally	53 34.6%	16 22.8%	3 22.6%	16 45.0%	20 37.0%
Frequently	24 15.9%	6 8.5%	0 3.1%	8 20.6%	16 29.3%
Total	152 100.0%	70 100.0%	12 100.0%	36 100.0%	53 100.0%

TABLE 5.4 Perception of INS Discrimination Against Latinos, by National Origin

Does INS Discriminate Against Latinos More Than Other Immigrant Ethnic Groups?	*Mexico*	*Cuba*	*Dominican Republic*	*Central America*	*South America*
Yes	187 26.8%	72 17.0%	22 21.3%	59 35.0%	74 34.5%
No	329 47.2%	247 57.9%	41 39.1%	68 40.0%	86 39.7%
Unsure	182 26.1%	107 25.1%	41 39.7%	42 25.0%	56 25.8%
Total	697 100.0%	426 100.0%	105 100.0%	169 100.0%	216 100.0%

Political Knowledge and Partisan Leanings

Findings

Among those Latino immigrants who tried to name the vice president, most answered correctly (Table 5.5). The rates of those who did not attempt to answer varied by national origin, with Mexican immigrants the most likely not to try.

Even fewer respondents were able to name the governor of their state (Table 5.6). Again, however, among those who tried most answered correctly.

With the two exceptions of Cubans and Central Americans, most of the non-U.S. citizens had not yet identified themselves with one of the political parties (Table 5.7). Among those respondents who expressed partisanship, not surprisingly Cubans were strongly Republican and Mexicans almost as strongly Democratic. Dominican and South American non-U.S. citizens with partisan attachments followed the Mexican model of two-to-one or greater support for the Democrats. Central Americans were more evenly divided, with a slight Republican bias.

Naturalized Cubans overwhelmingly reported Republican party adherence (Table 5.8). Naturalized Dominicans, and Mexicans to a slightly lesser degree, reported overwhelming support for the Democrats. Naturalized South Americans were slightly more likely to support the Republicans than they were to support the Democrats. Central Americans were split down the middle with a slight bias toward the Democrats.

Naturalized Latino citizens retained higher-than-average rates of lack of partisan affiliation. These rates ranged from 16 percent among Cubans to 33 percent among Mexicans.

Prior to the NLIS, little was known about the partisan leanings of Dominicans, Central Americans, and South Americans. These findings indicate that Dominicans follow the model of Mexicans, with strong Democratic partisanship. Central Americans and South Americans, on the other hand, reported more evenly divided levels of partisanship with strong levels of support for both parties. Yet, data from the NLIS demonstrate that for most Latino immigrants the process of partisan affiliation was not complete. Many Latino immigrants reported that they were unaffiliated.

Questions Asked: 51 and 57.
Tables with Comparable Data in Latino Voices: 5.10 and 8.24.

TABLE 5.5 Ability to Name the Vice President, by National Origin

Ability to Name Vice President	*Mexico*	*Cuba*	*Dominican Republic*	*Central America*	*South America*
Did not attempt	216 30.5%	43 9.9%	23 21.2%	28 16.5%	32 14.6%
Tried, but named incorrectly	31 4.4%	4 1.0%	3 2.3%	2 1.2%	3 1.3%
Named correctly	462 65.1%	382 89.1%	85 76.5%	142 82.3%	181 84.0%
Total	709 100.0%	429 100.0%	110 100.0%	172 100.0%	216 100.0%

TABLE 5.6 Ability to Name the Respondent's State Governor, by National Origin

Ability to Name Governor	*Mexico*	*Cuba*	*Dominican Republic*	*Central America*	*South America*
Did not attempt	373 52.6%	136 31.8%	52 47.5%	70 40.5%	56 25.9%
Tried, but named incorrectly	69 9.7%	11 2.6%	3 2.8%	10 5.6%	19 8.8%
Named correctly	267 37.7%	281 65.6%	55 49.7%	93 53.9%	141 65.3%
Total	709 100.0%	429 100.0%	110 100.0%	172 100.0%	216 100.0%

TABLE 5.7 Non-U.S.-Citizen Partisan Leanings, by National Origin

Partisan Leaning	*Mexico*	*Cuba*	*Dominican Republic*	*Central America*	*South America*
Republican	33 6.4%	98 50.1%	6 7.8%	27 27.1%	9 7.2%
Democrat	80 15.4%	14 7.1%	14 18.7%	22 22.0%	31 23.7%
Independent	35 6.8%	3 1.6%	2 2.2%	2 2.4%	20 15.2%
Other party	3 0.6%	0 0.2%	4 5.9%	0 0.0%	0 0.0%
Unaffiliated	366 70.8%	80 40.9%	50 65.4%	48 48.5%	71 53.9%
Total	517 100.0%	195 100.0%	76 100.0%	99 100.0%	132 100.0%

TABLE 5.8 U.S. Citizen Partisanship, by National Origin

Partisan Identification	*Mexico*	*Cuba*	*Dominican Republic*	*Central America*	*South America*
Republican	24 15.7%	144 63.0%	2 7.3%	20 33.4%	20 33.8%
Democrat	64 41.6%	19 8.5%	18 53.4%	22 35.2%	14 22.9%
Independent	15 10.1%	29 12.8%	2 5.1%	1 1.3%	13 21.2%
Other party	0 0.0%	0 0.0%	1 4.3%	0 0.0%	0 0.0%
Unaffiliated	50 32.7%	36 15.7%	10 29.9%	18 30.1%	13 22.1%
Total	153 100.0%	228 100.0%	33 100.0%	61 100.0%	61 100.0%

Political Participation

Findings

Among Latino immigrants who resided in their country of origin as adults, many participated in political activities (Table 5.9). While few voted, majorities of Dominicans, Central Americans, and South Americans participated in marches in their country of origin. A bare majority of Dominicans also followed home-country political news.

Across all measures of home-country political activities, Mexican immigrants were the least likely to be politically active and Dominicans the most likely.

The majority of each of the Latino national origin groups reported that they followed U.S. politics in the news (Table 5.10). With one exception, all other U.S. political activities saw few participants. The exception was contributing money or attending political fundraisers. The majority of Cubans and between 20 and 30 percent of Dominicans, Central Americans, and South Americans contributed money or attended fundraisers.

Among naturalized Latinos, the overwhelming majority of each of the national origin groups was registered to vote (Table 5.11). These registration rates exceeded 80 percent for all groups except for Mexicans, who had a 69 percent voter registration rate.

Among the registered voters, majorities of Mexicans, Cubans, and Central Americans voted in the most recent state election (Table 5.12). Mexicans had the highest voter turnout rate in the most recent state election.

Voter turnout in the most recent local election was not as high among naturalized Latino immigrants as it was for the most recent state election (Table 5.13). Mexicans were the only national origin group to have a majority that reported turning out. Dominicans and South Americans reported the lowest turnout rates.

School board elections saw even lower turnout rates (Table 5.14). Central Americans and Mexicans had the highest turnout rates and Dominicans the lowest for these elections.

Among those who had naturalized by 1984, a majority of each group but Mexicans voted in the presidential race (Table 5.15). Seventy-one percent of registered Cubans turned out in this race. The NLIS was conducted just prior to the 1988 campaign, so it is not possible to report voter turnout among the naturalized for the 1988 race.

Questions Asked: 46, 47, 49, 50, and 84a.
Tables with Comparable Data in Latino Voices: 8.11, 8.14, 8.17, and 8.23.

TABLE 5.9 Participation in Home-Country Political Activity, Among Respondents Who Migrated as Adults, by National Origin

Type of Home-Country Political Activity	*Mexico*	*Cuba*	*Dominican Republic*	*Central America*	*South America*
Followed political news	105 25.4% (n=413)	122 40.9% (n=298)	47 50.4% (n=93)	41 34.9% (n=119)	73 44.0% (n=167)
Marched	157 37.3% (n=413)	95 32.0% (n=298)	65 70.0% (n=93)	66 55.7% (n=119)	92 55.4% (n=167)
Voted	16 3.9% (n=413)	38 12.8% (n=298)	8 8.8% (n=93)	5 4.3% (n=119)	11 6.5% (n=167)

TABLE 5.10 Participation in U.S. Political Activity, by National Origin

Type of U. S. Political Activity	*Mexico*	*Cuba*	*Dominican Republic*	*Central America*	*South America*
Followed political news	383 54.1% (n=708)	265 61.9% (n=428)	61 55.9% (n=109)	95 58.2% (n=164)	133 61.7% (n=216)
Wrote letters about U.S. political issues	51 7.3% (n=707)	53 12.3% (n=428)	6 5.3% (n=109)	11 6.6% (n=167)	20 9.4% (n=216)
Distributed leaflets about political issues	32 4.5% (n=704)	40 9.5% (n=427)	3 2.7% (n=109)	12 6.9% (n=167)	3 1.6% (n=216)
Marched	40 5.7% (n=705)	65 15.2% (n=428)	6 5.3% (n=109)	15 9.3% (n=163)	13 5.8% (n=216)
Contributed money or attended fundraisers	99 15.3% (n=651)	221 52.4% (n=422)	31 28.5% (n=108)	47 28.7% (n=163)	46 21.7% (n=212)
Voted	55 7.9% (n=692)	71 16.5% (n=428)	9 8.2% (n=110)	11 6.2% (n=170)	20 9.1% (n=216)
Helped people register to vote	19 2.7% (n=700)	25 5.8% (n=428)	10 8.8% (n=110)	1 0.8% (n=167)	4 1.7% (n=216)

TABLE 5.11 Voter Registration Among U.S. Citizens, by National Origin

Registered to Vote in the United States	*Mexico*	*Cuba*	*Dominican Republic*	*Central America*	*South America*
Yes	110 69.3%	205 88.0%	28 86.2%	49 81.3%	53 82.7%
No	49 30.7%	28 12.0%	5 13.8%	11 18.7%	11 17.3%
Total	159 100.0%	232 100.0%	33 100.0%	60 100.0%	64 100.0%

TABLE 5.12 Voter Turnout Among Registered Voters in Most Recent State Election, by National Origin

Voted in the Last State Election	*Mexico*	*Cuba*	*Dominican Republic*	*Central America*	*South America*
Yes	69 63.3%	129 63.1%	13 44.9%	28 56.3%	25 47.5%
No	40 36.7%	75 36.9%	16 55.1%	21 43.7%	28 52.5%
Total	109 100.0%	205 100.0%	28 100.0%	49 100.0%	53 100.0%

TABLE 5.13 Voter Turnout Among Registered Voters in the Most Recent Local Election, by National Origin

Voted in the Last Local Election	*Mexico*	*Cuba*	*Dominican Republic*	*Central America*	*South America*
Yes	61 56.4%	96 46.9%	9 31.9%	21 43.1%	20 37.6%
No	47 43.6%	109 53.1%	19 68.1%	28 56.9%	33 62.4%
Total	109 100.0%	205 100.0%	28 100.0%	49 100.0%	53 100.0%

TABLE 5.14 Voter Turnout Among Registered Voters in the Most Recent School Board Election, by National Origin

Voted in the Last School Board Election	*Mexico*	*Cuba*	*Dominican Republic*	*Central America*	*South America*
Yes	40 36.9%	39 19.3%	1 5.0%	21 42.0%	14 25.5%
No	68 63.1%	165 80.7%	27 95.0%	28 58.0%	40 74.5%
Total	109 100.0%	205 100.0%	28 100.0%	49 100.0%	53 100.0%

TABLE 5.15 Voter Turnout in the 1984 Presidential Election Among Registered Voters Who Had Naturalized by 1984, by National Origin

Voted in the 1984 Presidential Election	*Mexico*	*Cuba*	*Dominican Republic*	*Central America*	*South America*
Yes	58 37.6%	135 70.7%	16 56.5%	22 52.9%	29 52.0%
No	96 62.4%	56 29.3%	12 43.5%	20 47.1%	27 48.0%
Total	153 100.0%	191 100.0%	29 100.0%	42 100.0%	57 100.0%

6

Attachment to the United States and Experiences with Naturalization

In this chapter, we focus on the process of immigrants becoming American citizens, of doing what Alejandro Portes has called "changing flags." Changing flags has both psychological and behavioral dimensions for immigrants. Psychologically, they develop attitudes of attachment to the nation and to the political system. Behaviorally, they must take specific actions to negotiate the bureaucratic steps necessary in order to naturalize.

As we indicate, most NLIS respondents had developed the behavioral and psychological attachments to the United States. The great majority intended to reside in the United States for the remainder of their lives and saw U.S. citizenship as a worthwhile goal. Yet, they held complex and often conflicting attitudes about national identification. Despite viewing U.S. citizenship as a positive value, a significant share of NLIS respondents maintained an identification with the country of origin.

For many NLIS respondents, the aspirations of integrating politically into American society had not been realized. Partially to blame for this are the complex and often confusing bureaucratic steps necessary to naturalize. We spend much of this chapter examining each of these steps and what impact each has on the immigrant who desires citizenship.

The Naturalization Application Process

The application process for citizenship has three formal steps—application, examination, and award. The first two steps present many potential obstacles for applicants. Obtaining and completing the application eliminates many potential citizens. Among those who successfully file the application and reach the examination stage, most succeed and become citizens. Yet, even at that stage, some do not succeed in reaching their goal.

Attachment to the United States

Findings

Almost to a one, Latino immigrants planned to make the United States their permanent home (Table 6.1).

Strong majorities of each of the Latino national origin groups asserted that life was better in the United States than in their country of origin (Table 6.2). Conversely, Cubans and South Americans were the most likely to say that life was better in the home country.

Latino immigrants were divided over the question of national identification (Table 6.3). Regardless of national origin, Latinos were more likely to identify with their country of origin than with the United States. These home-country identifiers included the majority of Mexicans and Central Americans. Yet, between 36 and 49 percent of respondents identified more with the United States than with their homeland. With all groups but the Cubans, these rates exceeded the rates for the naturalized from each national origin group (Table 3.60).

Almost universally, Latino immigrants expected their children's standard of living to be better than their own (Table 6.4).

Questions Asked: 10, 42, 52, and 53.
Tables with Comparable Data in Latino Voices: 2.33, 6.1, 6.2, and 10.31.

TABLE 6.1 Plans to Make a Permanent Home of the United States, by National Origin

Plans to Make a Permanent Home of the United States	*Mexico*	*Cuba*	*Dominican Republic*	*Central America*	*South America*
Yes	681 98.1%	422 99.8%	109 100.0%	165 97.0%	198 92.7%
No	13 1.9%	1 0.2%	0 0.0%	5 3.0%	16 7.3%
Total	694 100.0%	423 100.0%	109 100.0%	170 100.0%	214 100.0%

TABLE 6.2 Evaluation of Where Life is Better, by National Origin

Where Life is Better	*Mexico*	*Cuba*	*Dominican Republic*	*Central America*	*South America*
In the United States	582 84.3%	310 73.8%	94 85.4%	132 80.3%	141 67.5%
In country of origin	36 5.2%	76 18.2%	11 9.7%	18 11.1%	35 16.7%
In another place	73 10.5%	34 8.0%	5 4.9%	14 8.6%	33 15.8%
Total	691 100.0%	420 100.0%	110 100.0%	165 100.0%	209 100.0%

TABLE 6.3 National Self-Identification, by National Origin

National Self-Identification	*Mexico*	*Cuba*	*Dominican Republic*	*Central America*	*South America*
With the United States	250 36.4%	176 41.5%	54 49.4%	69 42.3%	85 41.0%
With the country of origin	396 57.7%	200 47.4%	52 47.9%	84 51.8%	103 49.9%
With some other country	40 5.9%	47 11.1%	3 2.7%	9 5.8%	19 9.1%
Total	686 100.0%	423 100.0%	109 100.0%	162 100.0%	206 100.0%

TABLE 6.4 Anticipations for Children's Lifestyle, by National Origin

Expected Lifestyle of Children	*Mexico*	*Cuba*	*Dominican Republic*	*Central America*	*South America*
Better than respondent	477 91.0%	279 93.8%	73 92.4%	96 89.7%	127 85.7%
Same as respondent	39 7.4%	13 4.5%	4 5.6%	9 8.2%	10 6.5%
Worse than respondent	8 1.6%	5 1.7%	2 2.0%	2 2.1%	11 7.7%
Total	524 100.0%	298 100.0%	79 100.0%	107 100.0%	149 100.0%

Attitudes Toward Naturalization

Findings

Contrary to conventional wisdom, the majority of Latino immigrants attached a high value to becoming a U.S. citizen. More than 60 percent of each national origin group rated becoming a U.S. citizen as "very" important (Table 6.5). Cubans and Dominicans were the most likely to rank citizenship in this manner. At the other extreme, between 3 and 5 percent of respondents rated becoming a U.S. citizen as "not at all" important.

Non-citizen respondents discussed U.S. citizenship with their friends and peers (Table 6.6). The most likely parties to initiate this discussion were the respondents' families, over half of whom had discussed U.S. citizenship. Peers were the next most likely. Overall, Cubans and South Americans were the most likely to report that people had discussed citizenship with them.

The preponderance of positive attitudes towards U.S. citizenship reflected the attitudes not only of the respondents but also of their peers. Almost universally, people who discussed U.S. citizenship with the non-citizen respondents favored naturalization (Tables 6.7, 6.8, 6.9, and 6.10).

Reasons for Becoming a U.S. Citizen

The NLIS asked two types of questions concerning reasons for naturalizing. The first of these was a ranking of various reasons given in the literature for naturalizing. Interestingly, when asked to evaluate the importance of ten factors associated with becoming an American citizen, respondents most often answered that attaining voting rights was a very important reason for naturalizing (Table 6.11). The next most often mentioned very important reason was increasing opportunities for children. The reason least likely to be evaluated as very important was increasing the opportunity to earn money.

When asked to provide the single most important reason for naturalizing, a plurality of respondents indicated that U.S. citizenship allowed immigrants to participate more fully in American life (Table 6.12). Nearly 40 percent of Dominicans offered this response.

Next in importance was the ability to participate in American politics and to become eligible for specific government programs. More than any of the other national origin groups, Cuban immigrants were likely to indicate that the most important reason for naturalizing was to express gratitude to the United States.

Few respondents had no opinion on the most important reason for naturalizing. Between half and two-thirds of respondents offered no second most important reason for naturalizing (Table 6.13).

Reasons for Not Becoming a U.S. Citizen

When asked to evaluate nine possible reasons for not naturalizing, non-citizen Latinos most often agreed that the statement that there are no benefits in naturalization was a very important reason for not naturalizing (Table 6.14). The second most often mentioned very important reason was a fear of the difficulty of the naturalization exam. The reason least often evaluated as very important was the plan to live permanently in the home country.

How immigrants rated the importance of different reasons for not naturalizing varied by national origin. Majorities of Cubans, Central Americans, and South Americans said that the absence of perceived benefits in naturalization was a very important reason for not naturalizing. A majority of Cubans gave as a reason the difficulty of the U.S. citizenship exam. The majority of Central Americans identified the discrimination faced by Latinos in the United States.

When non-citizens were asked to identify the single most important reason for not naturalizing, the most common response was simply not having considered it (Table 6.15). The second and third most common responses were provided by less than one-third as many respondents—love of home country and no reason to naturalize.

Approximately 40 percent of South Americans and Mexican immigrants who had not naturalized had never considered it as an option. Among Cubans, Dominicans, and Central Americans, just one-quarter had never considered it.

Questions Asked: 65, 91, 92, 92a, 97, 98, and 102.
Tables with Comparable Data in Latino Voices: None.

TABLE 6.5 Importance of Becoming a U.S. Citizen, by National Origin

Importance of Becoming a U.S. Citizen	*Mexico*	*Cuba*	*Dominican Republic*	*Central America*	*South America*
Very	426 61.6%	329 76.7%	84 76.9%	108 62.7%	128 61.0%
Somewhat	166 24.0%	67 15.7%	21 19.1%	32 18.7%	49 23.2%
Not very	79 11.5%	10 2.2%	1 1.3%	28 16.0%	22 10.6%
Not at all	20 2.9%	23 5.3%	3 2.7%	4 2.6%	11 5.2%
Total	693 100.0%	429 100.0%	109 100.0%	172 100.0%	210 100.0%

TABLE 6.6 Discussion of U.S. Citizenship with Non-Citizens, by National Origin

Who Had Discussed Citizenship with Non-Citizen Respondents?	*Mexico*	*Cuba*	*Dominican Republic*	*Central America*	*South America*
Family	324 59.2% (n=548)	117 59.8% (n=196)	44 57.2% (n=78)	56 51.0% (n=110)	111 73.7% (n=151)
Peers	234 42.7% (n=548)	122 61.9% (n=196)	35 45.7% (n=78)	49 44.9% (n=110)	70 46.4% (n=150)
Boss	59 10.9% (n=544)	49 25.5% (n=191)	7 9.4% (n=78)	17 15.5% (n=110)	34 22.5% (n=151)
Clergy	42 7.7% (n=548)	42 21.4% (n=196)	2 2.5% (n=78)	8 7.3% (n=110)	7 4.6% (n=150)
Others	26 4.7% (n=548)	31 15.8% (n=196)	5 7.1% (n=78)	7 6.2% (n=110)	10 6.8% (n=151)

TABLE 6.7 Peers' Attitudes Toward Respondent Naturalizing, Among Those Non-citizens Who Had Discussed Naturalization, by National Origin

Peers' Attitudes Toward Respondent Naturalizing	*Mexico*	*Cuba*	*Dominican Republic*	*Central America*	*South America*
Favor	203 86.7%	100 82.9%	33 93.7%	45 92.1%	69 98.6%
Oppose	9 3.7%	18 14.9%	1 4.0%	2 3.8%	0 0.0%
Mixed views	23 9.6%	3 2.3%	1 2.3%	2 4.1%	1 1.4%
Total	234 100.0%	121 100.0%	35 100.0%	49 100.0%	70 100.0%

TABLE 6.8 Bosses' Attitudes Toward Respondent Naturalizing, Among Those Non-citizens Who Had Discussed Naturalization, by National Origin

Bosses' Attitudes Toward Respondent Naturalizing	*Mexico*	*Cuba*	*Dominican Republic*	*Central America*	*South America*
Favor	59 98.7%	48 97.5%	7 92.6%	17 97.0%	27 80.2%
Oppose	0 0.6%	0 0.0%	1 7.4%	0 0.0%	7 19.8%
Mixed views	0 0.6%	1 2.5%	0 0.0%	1 3.0%	0 0.0%
Total	59 100.0%	49 100.0%	7 100.0%	17 100.0%	34 100.0%

TABLE 6.9 Clergy's Attitude Toward Respondent Naturalizing, Among Those Non-citizens Who Had Discussed Naturalization, by National Origin

Clergy's Attitude Toward Respondent Naturalizing	*Mexico*	*Cuba*	*Dominican Republic*	*Central America*	*South America*
Favors	42 100.0%	41 99.0%	2 100.0%	8 100.0%	7 100.0%
Opposes	0 0.0%	0 1.0%	0 0.0%	0 0.0%	0 0.0%
Total	42 100.0%	41 100.0%	2 100.0%	8 100.0%	7 100.0%

TABLE 6.10 Others' Attitudes Toward Respondent Naturalizing, Among Those Non-citizens Who Had Discussed Naturalization, by National Origin

Others' Attitudes Toward Respondent Naturalizing	*Mexico*	*Cuba*	*Dominican Republic*	*Central America*	*South America*
Favor	22 87.2%	31 100.0%	5 100.0%	3 39.3%	8 84.8%
Oppose	1 5.5%	0 0.0%	0 0.0%	0 0.0%	0 0.0%
Mixed views	2 7.3%	0 0.0%	0 0.0%	4 60.7%	2 15.2%
Total	25 100.0%	31 100.0%	5 100.0%	7 100.0%	10 100.0%

TABLE 6.11 Reasons for Seeking U.S. Citizenship, by National Origin

Reason (Ranked as Very Important)	*Mexico*	*Cuba*	*Dominican Republic*	*Central America*	*South America*
Naturalization allows the vote	597 86.4% (n=691)	399 93.1% (n=429)	102 92.3% (n=110)	158 93.8% (n=168)	172 80.5% (n=213)
Naturalization increases opportunities for children	546 79.3% (n=689)	335 79.1% (n=424)	99 89.5% (n=110)	143 83.4% (n=171)	156 74.3% (n=210)

(continues)

TABLE 6.11 *(continued)*

Reason (Ranked as Very Important)	*Mexico*	*Cuba*	*Dominican Republic*	*Central America*	*South America*
Naturalization helps relatives immigrate	525 75.4% (n=696)	340 79.8% (n=426)	91 83.5% (n=109)	141 82.9% (n=170)	154 72.3% (n=213)
Naturalization offers additional legal protections	523 75.1% (n=696)	319 75.4% (n=424)	99 91.0% (n=109)	135 80.3% (n=168)	138 66.4% (n=208)
Naturalization gives children citizenship	505 72.4% (n=698)	329 78.2% (n=421)	87 80.0% (n=108)	124 72.3% (n=172)	138 65.3% (n=211)
Naturalization expands job opportunities	524 74.9% (n=700)	281 67.5% (n=416)	93 84.1% (n=110)	124 72.3% (n=171)	124 58.2% (n=213)
Naturalization establishes eligibility for government programs	489 70.1% (n=698)	298 69.7% (n=427)	87 79.7% (n=109)	129 76.7% (n=168)	134 63.1% (n=212)
Naturalization allows equal participation in American life	469 67.9% (n=692)	295 69.3% (n=425)	96 88.2% (n=109)	129 74.9% (n=172)	130 61.2% (n=212)
Naturalization improves life in general	458 65.5% (n=699)	285 68.6% (n=416)	90 82.5% (n=109)	124 72.1% (n=172)	113 54.0% (n=210)
Naturalization increases opportunities to earn money	416 59.9% (n=695)	218 53.5% (n=408)	76 69.0% (n=110)	99 57.9% (n=171)	75 35.9% (n=208)

TABLE 6.12 Most Important Reason for Naturalizing, by National Origin

Most Important Reason for Naturalizing	*Mexico*	*Cuba*	*Dominican Republic*	*Central America*	*South America*
To participate more fully in American life	184 26.0%	141 33.0%	43 39.1%	42 24.4%	42 19.4%
To participate in American politics	110 15.5%	81 19.0%	4 3.4%	37 21.8%	36 16.9%
To express gratitude to the United States	21 3.0%	89 20.7%	8 6.9%	18 10.6%	17 7.7%
To attain eligibility for specific benefits	129 18.2%	21 4.8%	17 15.4%	15 8.9%	33 15.4%
To achieve economic opportunities	81 11.4%	16 3.7%	4 3.7%	21 12.1%	19 8.8%
To help children	18 2.6%	0 0.1%	1 1.3%	5 2.7%	5 2.3%
To assure a better life	61 8.5%	11 2.5%	8 6.9%	13 7.5%	13 6.2%
To resolve own or family's immigration problems	20 2.8%	11 2.5%	11 9.8%	13 7.4%	3 1.5%
To reduce discrimination	2 0.4%	4 0.9%	2 1.9%	1 0.3%	0 0.2%
There is no reason to naturalize	23 3.3%	20 4.6%	0 0.4%	3 1.7%	13 5.9%
No opinion	59 8.3%	35 8.2%	12 11.3%	4 2.5%	34 15.7%
Total	709 100.0%	429 100.0%	110 100.0%	172 100.0%	216 100.0%

TABLE 6.13 Second Most Important Reason for Naturalizing, by National Origin

Second Most Important Reason for Naturalizing	*Mexico*	*Cuba*	*Dominican Republic*	*Central America*	*South America*
To participate more fully in American life	53 7.5%	59 13.8%	14 13.0%	14 7.9%	26 12.1%
To participate in American politics	66 9.3%	34 7.9%	5 4.7%	14 8.2%	12 5.7%
To express gratitude to the United States	4 0.5%	34 7.8%	1 1.3%	2 1.0%	3 1.6%
To attain eligibility for specific benefits	48 6.7%	9 2.1%	4 3.8%	19 11.0%	21 9.9%
To achieve economic opportunities	56 7.9%	12 2.8%	5 4.4%	11 6.6%	9 4.3%
To help children	6 0.8%	1 0.2%	1 1.0%	1 0.9%	7 3.3%
To assure a better life	16 2.3%	5 1.2%	2 1.7%	6 3.5%	4 2.0%
To resolve own or family's immigration problems	12 1.7%	13 3.0%	5 4.6%	13 7.7%	1 0.4%
To reducediscrimination	6 0.8%	4 0.8%	0 0.4%	2 1.1%	3 1.2%
No second reason	442 62.4%	259 60.3%	72 65.1%	90 52.1%	129 59.6%
Total	709 100.0%	429 100.0%	110 100.0%	172 100.0%	216 100.0%

TABLE 6.14 Reasons for Not Seeking U.S. Citizenship Among Those Who Have Not Naturalized, by National Origin

Reason (Ranked as Very Important)	*Mexico*	*Cuba*	*Dominican Republic*	*Central America*	*South America*
Perception that there are no benefits in naturalization	130 25.1% (n=517)	62 32.4% (n=192)	21 28.7% (n=74)	44 42.0% (n=104)	47 32.2% (n=146)
Difficulty of U.S. citizenship exam	118 22.3% (n=529)	63 33.2% (n=190)	16 20.4% (n=78)	25 24.2% (n=103)	29 19.6% (n=149)
Latinos face discrimination in the United States	91 17.4% (n=524)	33 16.9% (n=193)	17 22.2% (n=75)	30 28.5% (n=104)	35 23.8% (n=148)
Desire to keep land in home country	110 20.8% (n=532)	13 6.6% (n=194)	13 17.1% (n=76)	18 17.4% (n=106)	23 15.5% (n=147)
Feelings of disloyalty to home country	44 8.6% (n=520)	44 22.5% (n=195)	19 25.0% (n=76)	27 25.0% (n=109)	16 11.0% (n=149)
Maintenance of political ties with country of origin	71 13.2% (n=537)	29 15.0% (n=194)	13 16.6% (n=78)	18 17.7% (n=104)	9 6.0% (n=149)
Fear of loss of culture	52 9.6% (n=539)	37 18.9% (n=195)	8 10.7% (n=75)	15 14.3% (n=104)	13 8.9% (n=151)
Fear of INS mistreatment	41 7.7% (n=530)	11 5.7% (n=194)	9 12.1% (n=76)	13 13.4% (n=100)	12 8.7% (n=138)
Plan to live permanently in home country	29 5.5% (n=525)	10 4.9% (n=195)	5 6.9% (n=78)	22 21.0% (n=103)	20 13.7% (n=149)

TABLE 6.15 Most Important Reason for Not Seeking Naturalization, Among Non-U.S.-Citizens, by National Origin

Most Important Reason for Not Naturalizing	*Mexico*	*Cuba*	*Dominican Republic*	*Central America*	*South America*
Has not considered	203 38.1%	48 25.0%	23 28.2%	23 22.8%	54 42.3%
Love of home country	47 8.7%	31 16.0%	7 8.2%	17 17.2%	11 8.6%
No reason to naturalize	70 13.2%	12 6.1%	7 9.0%	6 5.6%	7 5.2%
Does not speak English	56 10.4%	15 8.0%	11 13.9%	11 10.3%	6 5.0%
Intends to return to country of origin	21 3.9%	8 4.0%	5 5.9%	12 11.6%	13 9.8%
Believes that it is not possible to naturalize	37 6.9%	9 4.8%	5 6.2%	8 7.7%	6 4.4%
Desires to maintain property in home country	21 4.0%	2 1.0%	1 1.8%	2 2.2%	11 8.6%
Other	2 0.4%	12 6.0%	0 0.0%	4 4.4%	3 2.7%
None	76 14.3%	56 29.0%	22 26.7%	19 18.3%	17 13.4%
Total	532 100.0%	192 100.0%	81 100.0%	102 100.0%	129 100.0%

Preparation for Naturalization

Findings

Few respondents took English classes specifically to prepare for the naturalization exam (Table 6.16). Cuban immigrants were the most likely to have taken English classes for this purpose.

The majority of Cuban, Central American, and South American immigrants had taken U.S. history and civics classes since migrating to the United States (Table 6.17). For the most part, however, they did not take these classes to prepare for the naturalization exam (Table 6.18).

With the exception of South Americans, the majority of non-citizen respondents reported that they did not know the cost of naturalization (Table 6.19). Of those who ventured an estimate, a majority offered estimates in the correct range—less than $100 (at the time, naturalization cost $50). Interestingly, some non-U.S.-citizens were unaware that naturalization cost money at all.

Few non-U.S.-citizens anticipated that they would face denial if they applied for naturalization (Table 6.20). At the high end of the range, slightly more than 20 percent of South Americans perceived that they would face denial.

The majority of Latino immigrants perceived that the Immigration and Naturalization Service is helpful to applicants for U.S. citizenship (Table 6.21).

Questions Asked: 64, 64a, 94, 95, and 99.
Tables with Comparable Data in Latino Voices: None.

TABLE 6.16 Study of English to Prepare for Naturalization, by National Origin

English Study to Prepare for Naturalization	*Mexico*	*Cuba*	*Dominican Republic*	*Central America*	*South America*
Has not taken English classes	270 38.1%	149 34.7%	49 44.2%	40 23.5%	53 24.5%
Has taken English classes, but not to prepare for citizenship	338 47.7%	195 45.4%	42 37.9%	105 60.7%	135 62.7%
Has taken English classes to prepare for U.S. citizenship	101 14.2%	86 20.0%	20 17.9%	27 15.8%	28 12.8%
Total	709 100.0%	429 100.0%	110 100.0%	172 100.0%	216 100.0%

TABLE 6.17 Study of U.S. History and Civics, by National Origin

U.S. History and Civics Study	*Mexico*	*Cuba*	*Dominican Republic*	*Central America*	*South America*
Yes	313 44.2%	251 58.5%	26 23.7%	104 60.2%	118 54.9%
No	394 55.8%	178 41.5%	84 76.3%	69 39.8%	97 45.1%
Total	707 100.0%	429 100.0%	110 100.0%	172 100.0%	216 100.0%

TABLE 6.18 Study of U.S. History and Civics to Prepare for Naturalization, by National Origin

U.S. History and Civics Study to Prepare for Naturalization	*Mexico*	*Cuba*	*Dominican Republic*	*Central America*	*South America*
Yes	141 20.0%	125 29.1%	12 11.1%	38 22.1%	41 19.1%
No	171 24.1%	126 29.5%	14 12.6%	66 38.1%	77 35.9%
Has not taken history or civics classes	397 56.0%	178 41.5%	84 76.3%	69 39.8%	97 45.1%
Total	709 100.0%	429 100.0%	110 100.0%	172 100.0%	216 100.0%

TABLE 6.19 Estimates of Cost of Applying for Naturalization, Among Those Who Have Not Applied, by National Origin

Estimated Cost of Naturalization	*Mexico*	*Cuba*	*Dominican Republic*	*Central America*	*South America*
Less than $100	109 21.7%	57 34.2%	20 26.5%	14 14.7%	45 34.9%
$100-$200	25 5.0%	11 6.5%	5 6.3%	7 7.2%	12 9.6%
$201 or more	23 4.5%	6 3.5%	1 1.1%	6 6.0%	2 1.2%
Was not aware that it cost money	47 9.4%	6 3.7%	8 10.5%	7 8.0%	13 10.1%
Do not know	299 59.3%	87 52.0%	41 55.6%	59 64.1%	57 44.2%
Total	503 100.0%	167 100.0%	74 100.0%	92 100.0%	128 100.0%

Note: At the time of the survey, the cost of filing the naturalization application, the only governmental fee, was $50.00.

TABLE 6.20 Anticipation of Denial of Citizenship, Among Those Who Have Not Applied, by National Origin

Belief that Respondent Would Be Denied Citizenship	*Mexico*	*Cuba*	*Dominican Republic*	*Central America*	*South America*
Yes	76 13.9%	33 16.6%	11 13.0%	5 4.9%	33 22.0%
No	474 86.1%	166 83.4%	71 87.0%	100 95.1%	116 78.0%
Total	550 100.0%	199 100.0%	82 100.0%	105 100.0%	148 100.0%

TABLE 6.21 Perception of Availability of I.N.S. Naturalization Assistance, by National Origin

INS Treatment of Citizenship Applicants	*Mexico*	*Cuba*	*Dominican Republic*	*Central America*	*South America*
Helpful	419 59.2%	293 68.3%	72 65.1%	121 70.2%	124 57.3%
Unhelpful	88 12.4%	51 11.9%	3 2.4%	20 11.6%	42 19.3%
Neither	125 17.6%	65 15.2%	26 23.7%	16 9.2%	29 13.6%
No opinion	77 10.8%	20 4.6%	10 8.9%	16 9.0%	21 9.9%
Total	709 100.0%	429 100.0%	110 100.0%	172 100.0%	216 100.0%

The Application Process

Findings

The share of immigrants attempting to obtain the application form that formally begins the naturalization process varied by national origin (Table 6.22). More than 60 percent of Cuban immigrants eligible for citizenship and more than 50 percent of South Americans had made this step. Rates for Mexicans, Dominicans, and Central Americans were somewhat lower (38, 45, and 43 percent, respectively).

Most respondents were able to obtain the application on their own (Table 6.23). Among those who did seek outside help, most did not have to pay (Table 6.24). The exception to this pattern was Central Americans. Almost 60 percent of Central Americans who sought outside help to get the application paid for the form, which is free from the government. It should be noted that the numbers who sought outside help were small, so these findings should be interpreted cautiously.

Among those who paid to obtain the application form, most paid less than $10.00 (Table 6.25). Again, there was an exception. Of the ten South Americans who paid for the application, eight paid $50.00 or more!

With the exception of Cuban immigrants, the majority of each of the national origin groups initiated naturalization in the eight years prior to the survey (Table 6.26). The majority of Cubans who had initiated naturalization, on the other hand, began to apply in the 1970s and before.

Few Dominicans, Central Americans, or South Americans began to naturalize before the 1970s and more than two-thirds began in 1980s or after. These data indicate that naturalization among Latinos in general began to rise in the 1980s.

Among those Latino immigrants who had obtained the naturalization application, between 62 and 81 percent went on to file the application with the INS (Table 6.27). Cubans and Central Americans were the most likely to file applications once they obtained them.

Among those who tried to obtain the application form but had not filed it, the majority of each national origin group intended to in the future (Table 6.28). Among these, Mexicans and South Americans were the most likely to report this.

Respondents offered a variety of reasons for not applying for citizenship despite having obtained the application form (Table 6.29). Most important among these were the lack of time to prepare, the need to study English, and a lack of interest in obtaining U.S. citizenship.

Most applicants had applied for citizenship just once (Table 6.30). Nearly one-quarter of Dominicans and Central Americans, however, had applied more than once. Multiple applications are necessary when the INS returns applications for many reasons, such as failing to complete the application correctly, failing to meet the statutory requirements for citizenship, or failing the exam. At the time of the NLIS, applicants in this final category could appeal the administrative denial to the courts. A failure at the judicial level (a formal denial of the application) could also have resulted in a second application.

Among those who had not sought or obtained naturalization applications, majorities intended to apply at some time in the future (Table 6.31). Dominicans showed the highest rates of intended application and Cubans the lowest. In part, these low rates among Cubans reflect the large numbers who have already naturalized.

Questions Asked: 67, 70, 71, 73, 74, 75, 76, 77, and 93.
Tables with Comparable Data in Latino Voices: 2.34 and 10.18.

TABLE 6.22 Efforts to Obtain Naturalization Application, by National Origin

Tried to Obtain Application	*Mexico*	*Cuba*	*Dominican Republic*	*Central America*	*South America*
Yes	267 38.0%	257 60.1%	49 45.2%	74 42.9%	111 52.0%
No	435 62.0%	171 39.9%	60 54.8%	98 57.1%	103 48.0%
Total	701 100.0%	428 100.0%	109 100.0%	171 100.0%	214 100.0%

TABLE 6.23 How the Respondent Obtained the Application, by National Origin

How Did the Respondent Obtain the Application?	*Mexico*	*Cuba*	*Dominican Republic*	*Central America*	*South America*
Someone helped	94 36.6%	64 24.8%	19 38.7%	17 22.8%	35 31.9%
Respondent obtained on own	163 63.4%	193 75.2%	30 61.3%	57 77.2%	74 68.1%
Total	258 100.0%	257 100.0%	49 100.0%	73 100.0%	109 100.0%

TABLE 6.24 Need to Pay for Application, by National Origin

Did Respondent Have to Pay to Get the Application?	*Mexico*	*Cuba*	*Dominican Republic*	*Central America*	*South America*
Yes	27 28.4%	11 18.5%	6 33.1%	10 59.6%	12 37.4%
No	68 71.6%	50 81.5%	13 66.9%	7 40.4%	21 62.6%
Total	94 100.0%	62 100.0%	19 100.0%	17 100.0%	33 100.0%

TABLE 6.25 Cost of Obtaining Application Among Those Who Paid, by National Origin

How Much Did Respondent Pay to Get the Application?	*Mexico*	*Cuba*	*Dominican Republic*	*Central America*	*South America*
$10.00 or less	12 51.5%	6 78.4%	1 18.7%	5 52.3%	1 12.0%
$10.01-$49.99	9 40.3%	2 21.6%	3 57.2%	4 39.8%	1 10.9%
$50.00 or more	2 8.2%	0 0.0%	1 24.1%	1 7.9%	8 77.1%
Total	23 100.0%	7 100.0%	6 100.0%	10 100.0%	11 100.0%

TABLE 6.26 Decade in Which Applicants Began Application Process, by National Origin

Decade in Which Respondent Obtained the Application	*Mexico*	*Cuba*	*Dominican Republic*	*Central America*	*South America*
1960s or before	35 14.1%	49 20.5%	1 3.1%	8 10.5%	8 7.4%
1970s	48 19.3%	99 41.2%	10 22.6%	14 19.0%	28 26.5%
1980s	167 66.5%	92 38.4%	34 74.3%	51 70.5%	71 66.2%
Total	251 100.0%	241 100.0%	46 100.0%	72 100.0%	108 100.0%

TABLE 6.27 Filing of the Naturalization Application Among Those Who Tried to Get the Application, by National Origin

Has Respondent Filed Application with INS?	*Mexico*	*Cuba*	*Dominican Republic*	*Central America*	*South America*
Yes	164 61.9%	206 80.4%	30 61.7%	60 81.4%	73 65.4%
No	101 38.1%	50 19.6%	19 38.3%	14 18.6%	39 34.6%
Total	265 100.0%	257 100.0%	49 100.0%	74 100.0%	111 100.0%

TABLE 6.28 Plans to Apply for Naturalization, Among Those Who Tried to Obtain the Application but Had Not Filed, by National Origin

Plans to Apply for Citizenship	*Mexico*	*Cuba*	*Dominican Republic*	*Central America*	*South America*
Yes	86 87.4%	29 74.7%	13 80.0%	9 75.5%	31 88.3%
No	12 12.6%	10 25.3%	3 20.0%	3 24.5%	4 11.7%
Total	98 100.0%	39 100.0%	17 100.0%	13 100.0%	35 100.0%

TABLE 6.29 Reasons for Delaying Application, by National Origin

Reason	Mexico	Cuba	Dominican Republic	Central America	South America
No time to prepare	101 19.1%	25 13.7%	8 10.8%	12 14.3%	14 12.5%
Needs to study English	127 24.0%	41 22.5%	25 33.8%	6 7.0%	18 16.1%
Not interested in U.S. citizenship	41 7.7%	19 10.4%	11 14.9%	6 7.2%	27 24.1%
Fears the Immigration and Naturalization Service	8 1.5%	3 1.6%	2 2.5%	2 2.4%	0 0.0%
Never considered applying	56 10.6%	0 0.7%	0 0.0%	2 2.4%	7 6.3%
Does not want to lose home-country citizenship	21 4.0%	2 1.1%	3 4.1%	10 11.9%	15 13.4%
Not sure how to proceed	48 9.1%	18 9.9%	7 9.5%	16 19.0%	11 9.8%
Preparing for test	57 10.8%	32 17.6%	4 5.5%	8 9.5%	8 7.1%
Needs to study government and civics	29 5.5%	7 3.8%	2 2.5%	12 14.3%	4 3.4%
Form is too complicated	9 1.7%	18 9.9%	2 2.9%	1 1.2%	0 0.0%
Waiting for eligibility to take test in Spanish	20 3.8%	6 3.3%	8 10.8%	6 7.1%	4 3.4%
Other	13 2.2%	10 5.5%	2 2.7%	3 3.7%	4 3.9%
Total	530 100.0%	182 100.0%	74 100.0%	84 100.0%	112 100.0%

TABLE 6.30 Number of Times Respondent Has Applied, by National Origin

Number of Times Respondent Has Applied for Naturalization	*Mexico*	*Cuba*	*Dominican Republic*	*Central America*	*South America*
One	148 90.3%	187 91.4%	23 75.9%	55 91.9%	56 76.9%
Two or more	16 9.7%	18 8.6%	7 24.1%	5 8.1%	17 23.1%
Total	164 100.0%	205 100.0%	30 100.0%	60 100.0%	73 100.0%

TABLE 6.31 Plans to File Application in the Future, Among Those Who Have Not Obtained the Application, by National Origin

Plans to File Application in the Future	*Mexico*	*Cuba*	*Dominican Republic*	*Central America*	*South America*
Yes	292 75.5%	71 49.8%	52 88.8%	63 73.7%	63 72.7%
No	95 24.5%	72 50.2%	7 11.2%	22 26.3%	24 27.3%
Total	386 100.0%	143 100.0%	58 100.0%	85 100.0%	87 100.0%

The Examination Experience

Findings

Among those respondents who had applied for naturalization, more than half had taken the exam (Table 6.32). Dominicans had the highest examination rates. Few respondents had taken the exam more than once (Table 6.33).

Most respondents took their naturalization exam in the 1980s (Table 6.34). Again, Cubans who had taken the exam did so over a longer time period. Unexpectedly, considering the patterns of immigration, a handful of South Americans took their naturalization exam in or before the 1960s.

The average length of time between receiving the green card and taking the naturalization exam was ten years or less for all national origin groups except Mexicans, for whom the modal interval was between eleven and twenty years (Table 6.35). With the exception of approximately 20 percent of Mexican respondents, few immigrants who had allowed more than twenty-one years to elapse since receiving their green cards naturalized.

Reflecting the pervasiveness of residence in the United States prior to receiving the green card, the interval between immigration and citizenship exam exceeded the interval between the exam and the green card (Table 6.36). South Americans joined Mexicans with modal intervals of eleven to twenty years. Also, more than 25 percent of Mexicans, 19 percent of Central Americans, and 11 percent of Cubans allowed twenty-one or more years to elapse prior to naturalizing.

For the most part, Mexican respondents took their exam in California and Texas and Dominicans took their exam in New York (Table 6.37). The exam locations of the other Latino national origin groups were more dispersed.

Regardless of national origin, exam takers found the experience to be either "somewhat" easy or "very" easy (Table 6.38). The majority of Cuban and Central American exam takers and a near-majority of Mexicans found it "very" easy.

The majority of exam takers did not identify any specific part of the exam to be difficult (Table 6.39). Generally, they were more likely to find the history section more difficult than the English or writing sections.

Overwhelming majorities of each national origin group reported that the INS examiner was helpful (Table 6.40). Mexicans and Central Americans were the most likely to report rude examiners.

Few respondents took the exam in a language other than English (Table 6.41). At the time of the NLIS, applicants aged fifty-five or older who had lived in the United States for twenty or more years could choose to take the exam in their native language. These data indicate that relatively few availed themselves of this opportunity.

Examiners asked exam takers different numbers of questions (Table 6.42). The modal number was, however, less than eleven.

Almost universally, exam takers reported that the exam was fair (Table 6.43). Most passed their exam (Table 6.44). Dominicans had the highest failure rate, with more than one-quarter failing.

Among those who failed the exam or who were asked to refile their application in the face of potential denial, most Mexicans, Cubans, and Dominicans planned to reapply (Table 6.45). Although the numbers were small, just one-third of Central Americans and South Americans who did not succeed in their pursuit of citizenship reported that they would definitely restart their naturalization applications.

Overall, the majority of Mexicans, Cubans, and Dominicans and near-majorities of Central and South Americans reported that they had been "very" satisfied with their experiences with the INS (Table 6.46). Less than 5 percent reported that they were "very" dissatisfied.

Questions Asked: K, 6, 75, 82, 83, 84a, 84b, 84c, 84d, 84e, 84f, 84g, 84h, 84i, 85, and 101.
Tables with Comparable Data in Latino Voices: None.

TABLE 6.32 Exam Taken Among Those Who Applied, by National Origin

Exam Taken Among Those Who Applied	*Mexico*	*Cuba*	*Dominican Republic*	*Central America*	*South America*
Yes	113	165	23	48	55
	72.1%	80.8%	87.7%	79.9%	75.6%
No	44	39	3	12	18
	27.9%	19.2%	12.3%	20.1%	24.4%
Total	157	204	26	60	73
	100.0%	100.0%	100.0%	100.0%	100.0%

TABLE 6.33 Number of Times Exam Taken, by National Origin

Number of Times Citizenship Exam Taken	*Mexico*	*Cuba*	*Dominican Republic*	*Central America*	*South America*
One	104	160	19	43	41
	92.2%	97.6%	93.0%	88.8%	89.5%
Two or more	9	4	1	5	5
	7.8%	2.4%	7.0%	11.2%	10.5%
Total	113	164	20	48	46
	100.0%	100.0%	100.0%	100.0%	100.0%

TABLE 6.34 Period When Naturalization Exam was Taken, by National Origin

Period in Which Citizenship Exam Taken	*Mexico*	*Cuba*	*Dominican Republic*	*Central America*	*South America*
1960s or before	14	38	0	1	13
	13.0%	26.1%	0.0%	2.3%	23.5%
1970s	27	58	4	7	5
	24.5%	39.6%	19.4%	14.4%	10.2%
1980s	68	50	18	39	36
	62.5%	34.3%	80.6%	83.3%	66.4%
Total	109	146	22	47	54
	100.0%	100.0%	100.0%	100.0%	100.0%

TABLE 6.35 Period Between Receiving Green Card and Taking Naturalization Exam, by National Origin

Period Between Receiving Green Card and Citizenship Exam	*Mexico*	*Cuba*	*Dominican Republic*	*Central America*	*South America*
10 years or less	37	86	15	26	26
	41.5%	74.2%	73.9%	60.9%	65.3%
11-20	34	20	5	9	12
	37.5%	17.3%	26.1%	20.3%	29.7%
21 or more	19	10	0	8	2
	21.0%	8.5%	0.0%	18.8%	5.0%
Total	90	116	21	42	39
	100.0%	100.0%	100.0%	100.0%	100.0%

TABLE 6.36 Length of Time Between Immigration and Naturalization Exam, by National Origin

Period Between Immigration and Citizenship Exam	*Mexico*	*Cuba*	*Dominican Republic*	*Central America*	*South America*
10 years or less	38 38.2%	86 59.5%	13 59.6%	24 50.3%	18 40.3%
11-20	36 35.9%	43 29.9%	8 35.4%	14 30.7%	24 53.5%
21 or more	26 25.9%	15 10.5%	1 5.0%	9 19.0%	3 6.2%
Total	101 100.0%	144 100.0%	22 100.0%	47 100.0%	45 100.0%

TABLE 6.37 State of Naturalization Exam, by National Origin

State in Which Exam Taken	*Mexico*	*Cuba*	*Dominican Republic*	*Central America*	*South America*
California	55 51.7%	8 4.9%	0 1.9%	20 42.2%	11 22.6%
Florida	0 0.4%	77 47.2%	0 0.0%	2 3.4%	10 21.4%
Illinois	7 6.6%	10 6.0%	0 0.0%	0 0.0%	2 5.0%
New Jersey	0 0.0%	26 15.9%	4 17.3%	7 14.3%	7 14.8%
New York	5 4.5%	35 21.6%	16 80.8%	12 25.8%	15 30.5%
Texas	34 31.7%	2 1.5%	0 0.0%	7 14.1%	1 1.6%
Other	5 5.1%	5 3.0%	0 0.0%	0 0.0%	2 4.1%
Total	106 100.0%	163 100.0%	20 100.0%	46 100.0%	48 100.0%

TABLE 6.38 Difficulty of the Citizenship Exam, by National Origin

Difficulty of the Citizenship Exam	*Mexico*	*Cuba*	*Dominican Republic*	*Central America*	*South America*
Very hard	6 5.6%	19 11.8%	1 6.1%	3 5.6%	4 9.4%
Somewhat hard	16 13.9%	21 13.0%	4 18.2%	6 11.8%	8 17.2%
Somewhat easy	37 33.4%	36 21.9%	7 31.1%	13 26.4%	17 36.2%
Very easy	53 47.1%	87 53.3%	10 44.5%	27 56.2%	17 37.2%
Total	112 100.0%	163 100.0%	23 100.0%	48 100.0%	46 100.0%

TABLE 6.39 Aspects of the Exam Found to be Difficult, by National Origin

Difficult Aspects of the Exam	*Mexico*	*Cuba*	*Dominican Republic*	*Central America*	*South America*
English requirements	12 11.1% (n=109)	16 11.2% (n=146)	3 15.5% (n=22)	5 10.1% (n=47)	2 4.6% (n=54)
History requirements	36 32.7% (n=109)	48 32.7% (n=146)	9 41.4% (n=22)	9 19.5% (n=47)	15 28.5% (n=54)
Writing requirements	6 5.2% (n=109)	12 8.4% (n=146)	3 15.2% (n=22)	3 7.3% (n=47)	1 1.7% (n=54)
Completing the application	6 5.5% (n=109)	1 0.5% (n=146)	2 8.6% (n=22)	3 6.0% (n=47)	0 0.0% (n=54)
Other aspects of the exam	44 40.6% (n=109)	52 35.4% (n=146)	7 33.0% (n=22)	21 45.1% (n=47)	29 54.9% (n=54)

TABLE 6.40 Behavior of INS Examiner, by National Origin

Behavior of INS Examiner	*Mexico*	*Cuba*	*Dominican Republic*	*Central America*	*South America*
Helpful	91 81.6%	134 82.2%	21 89.2%	35 74.5%	38 70.3%
Rude	17 15.4%	8 4.8%	0 0.0%	7 13.8%	5 9.5%
Neutral	3 3.1%	21 13.0%	3 10.8%	6 11.7%	11 20.2%
Total	111 100.0%	163 100.0%	23 100.0%	48 100.0%	55 100.0%

TABLE 6.41 Language of Naturalization Exam, by National Origin

Language of Exam	*Mexico*	*Cuba*	*Dominican Republic*	*Central America*	*South America*
English	96 86.5%	161 98.5%	23 100.0%	46 96.8%	46 84.6%
Spanish	10 9.1%	0 0.2%	0 0.0%	1 1.6%	0 0.0%
Both	5 4.5%	2 1.3%	0 0.0%	1 1.6%	8 15.4%
Total	111 100.0%	164 100.0%	23 100.0%	48 100.0%	55 100.0%

TABLE 6.42 Number of Questions in Exam, by National Origin

Number of Questions Asked at the Exam	*Mexico*	*Cuba*	*Dominican Republic*	*Central America*	*South America*
1-10	67 61.4%	72 48.9%	15 68.7%	29 61.2%	28 51.8%
11-20	13 11.4%	10 6.8%	2 9.0%	12 25.4%	11 19.7%
21 or more	6 5.5%	4 2.8%	0 0.0%	0 0.0%	1 1.5%
Does not remember	24 21.7%	61 41.5%	5 22.3%	6 13.4%	14 27.0%
Total	109 100.0%	146 100.0%	22 100.0%	47 100.0%	54 100.0%

TABLE 6.43 Fairness of Exam Questions, by National Origin

Fairness of Questions	*Mexico*	*Cuba*	*Dominican Republic*	*Central America*	*South America*
Fair	104 94.2%	158 98.5%	19 93.0%	47 98.6%	53 100.0%
Not fair	6 5.8%	2 1.5%	1 7.0%	1 1.4%	0 0.0%
Total	110 100.0%	160 100.0%	20 100.0%	48 100.0%	53 100.0%

TABLE 6.44 Examination Pass Rate, by National Origin

Did Respondent Pass the Exam?	*Mexico*	*Cuba*	*Dominican Republic*	*Central America*	*South America*
Yes	100 88.1%	158 96.1%	17 74.9%	46 96.9%	48 88.8%
No	13 11.9%	6 3.9%	6 25.1%	1 3.1%	6 11.2%
Total	113 100.0%	165 100.0%	23 100.0%	48 100.0%	55 100.0%

TABLE 6.45 Plans to Take Exam Among Those Who Failed or Who Had Their Applications Returned by the INS, by National Origin

Plan to Take Exam Among Those Who Failed or Refiled Their Applications	*Mexico*	*Cuba*	*Dominican Republic*	*Central America*	*South America*
Yes	32 64.9%	30 70.0%	5 100.0%	4 32.8%	8 33.5%
No	11 21.9%	12 28.3%	0 0.0%	9 67.2%	11 49.8%
Unsure	6 13.2%	1 1.7%	0 0.0%	0 0.0%	4 16.7%
Total	49 100.0%	43 100.0%	5 100.0%	13 100.0%	23 100.0%

TABLE 6.46 Satisfaction with Treatment by INS, by National Origin

Overall Satisfaction with INS Services	*Mexico*	*Cuba*	*Dominican Republic*	*Central America*	*South America*
Very satisfied	433 62.2%	299 69.8%	70 63.5%	83 48.1%	102 48.0%
Somewhat satisfied	133 19.1%	70 16.3%	16 14.7%	49 28.7%	32 15.0%
Somewhat dissatisfied	27 3.8%	7 1.7%	3 2.3%	16 9.4%	32 15.2%
Very dissatisfied	19 2.7%	13 2.9%	2 2.0%	4 2.2%	10 4.9%
No experiences with the INS	85 12.2%	40 9.3%	19 17.5%	20 11.6%	36 17.0%
Total	696 100.0%	428 100.0%	110 100.0%	171 100.0%	212 100.0%

7

Selected Characteristics of Latino Immigrants by Stage in the Naturalization Process

In this chapter, we explore selected characteristics of Latino immigrants according to their stage in the naturalization process. Specifically, we examine the differences between eligible immigrants who had naturalized and those who had not. Among those who had not naturalized, we probe the differences, if any, between immigrants who had begun to naturalize and those who had not. As we will indicate, identifying those who had begun presents an analytical problem. As far as the Immigration and Naturalization Service is concerned, naturalization formally begins with the filing of the application. When the courts awarded naturalization, they defined an initiated application as one that the INS had reviewed and presented to the clerk of the court with a recommendation for an award or a denial. We find, on the other hand, that for the naturalizing immigrant, the application process actually begins somewhat earlier.

Because one of the foci of the National Latino Immigrant Survey was the bureaucratic process of naturalization, its results offer a previously unavailable picture of the dynamic between immigrants' attitudinal interest in naturalization and their behavioral efforts to attain that goal. Based on survey findings, we have developed an indicator that separates those who have taken behavioral acts to initiate naturalization from those who have not. This, we would argue, offers a better indicator than either the INS measure or the judicial measure of both the level of interest and the level of discouragement among immigrants seeking citizenship. Thus, if the naturalized represent one end of a continuum and those who have not tried to naturalize represent the other end, we find that there is a large middle category of immigrants who have tried and failed in their effort to naturalize.

Initiating Naturalization

In Chapter Six, we identified several possible indicators of the behavioral start of naturalization. Does it, for example, begin when the immigrant files the application for citizenship with the INS? According to the courts (at least at the time of the NLIS), it begins even later. We, on the other hand, use an earlier point in time as the formal beginning to the naturalization process. Specifically, we use either of two behavioral acts. The first is obtaining the naturalization application from the INS. The second is taking English language or civics classes with the intent of preparing for the naturalization exam. Thus, for the purposes of discussion, we place non-naturalized Latino immigrants in one of two categories—those who had not initiated the naturalization process and those who had.

We need to make one further distinction. As shown in Table 3.61, there are two forms of naturalization. The first is the one discussed throughout this volume and is the pattern that adult immigrants must follow. Although the pattern may vary slightly from immigrant to immigrant, the general pattern has the immigrant developing an attachment to the United States, preparing for the exam, completing the application, taking the test, and being sworn in as a U.S. citizen. Immigrant children, on the other hand, follow a different route to U.S. citizenship—they must follow the lead of their parents. Regardless of their attachment to the United States, immigrants younger than eighteen years of age can only naturalize if their parents do (and if the parents complete the appropriate paperwork to include their children in the process). The INS characterizes these minors who naturalize as "derivative" citizens. Thus, immi-

TABLE 7.1 Stage in the Naturalization Process, by National Origin

Stage	*Mexico*	*Cuba*	*Dominican Republic*	*Central America*	*South America*
Has not begun	332 51.1%	96 25.7%	48 46.5%	53 35.5%	72 38.0%
Begun, not completed	205 31.6%	101 27.2%	34 32.8%	49 32.7%	64 34.1%
Naturalized citizen	112 17.3%	175 47.1%	21 20.7%	48 31.8%	52 27.9%
Total	650 100.0%	372 100.0%	103 100.0%	149 100.0%	188 100.0%

Note: This table excludes derivative citizens (see Table 3.61).

grant children who naturalize prior to adulthood must depend on the interests and attitudes of their parents and do not themselves have to go through the attitudinal changes or behavioral actions that we would argue must accompany naturalization.

The number of derivative citizens is not insignificant. According to the NLIS, 8.9 percent of Latino immigrants with the length of residence necessary to naturalize have become U.S. citizens through the actions of their parents. Fully one in four naturalized Latinos is a derivative U.S. citizen. Yet, for the reasons cited, we exclude the derivative citizens from the analysis in this chapter. Table 7.1 indicates the share of each of the Latino immigrant national origin groups in the stages in the path from immigrant to citizen (excluding derivative citizens).

Social and Demographic Characteristics of Immigrants

Findings

Women and men were found in similar proportions in each stage of the naturalization process (Table 7.2).

Older respondents were more likely to be naturalized (Table 7.3). Age did not appear to distinguish those who had not initiated naturalization from those who had initiated but not completed the naturalization process.

Naturalized citizens were more likely than the non-naturalized to have college degrees (Table 7.4). At the other extreme, more than half of those who had not begun to naturalize had eight or fewer years of education.

A greater share of the naturalized had higher incomes than the non-naturalized (Table 7.5). Income did not distinguish those non-citizens who had initiated naturalization from those who had not. While the income-related differences between naturalized and non-naturalized remained when we examined per capita household income, they narrowed considerably (Table 7.6).

The naturalized were slightly more likely to be found in the labor force than the non-naturalized (Table 7.7). The difference resulted from a higher share of the non-naturalized being temporarily unemployed. Approximately one-third of the respondents, regardless of naturalization status, were not in the labor force.

Those who had not initiated naturalization were more likely than either those who had begun to naturalize or the naturalized to be found in low-status occupations, such as laborers, farm laborers, and operatives (Table 7.8). Fully one-fifth of naturalized citizens held professional positions.

The naturalized were more likely than the non-naturalized to own their own home (Table 7.9). Nearly half of the non-citizens, however, were homeowners.

Among those who had not initiated naturalization and among the naturalized citizens, the modal length of residence in the same area was eleven to twenty years (Table 7.10). Those who had initiated but not completed naturalization were equally likely to have lived in the same area for one to five years as they were to have done so for eleven to twenty years.

Regardless of naturalization interest or status, few Latino immigrants spoke English exclusively at home (Table 7.11). Approximately one-quarter of the naturalized spoke both English and Spanish at home.

The majority of the naturalized reported that they spoke English either well or very well (Table 7.12). Just 25 percent of those who had not initiated naturalization and 42 percent of those in the process of naturalizing reported similar English speaking abilities.

Rates for self-reported English listening comprehension were generally higher than those for English speaking ability (Table 7.13). The majority of both the naturalized and those in the process of naturalizing reported that they understood English either well or very well.

In terms of English writing ability, the majority of naturalized citizens and 21 percent of those who had not initiated reported that they write well or very well (Table 7.14). Among those in the process of naturalizing, 38 percent reported that they could write well or very well.

Again, the naturalized were more likely to report stronger abilities to read in English than were the non-citizens (Table 7.15). Among the non-naturalized, those who had initiated citizenship were more likely than those who had not initiated it to report that they read English either well or very well.

More than four in five of the naturalized had studied English since immigration (Table 7.16). More than three-quarters of respondents in the process of naturalizing and almost half of those who had not begun to apply had studied English since coming to the United States.

The modal decade of immigration for the naturalized was the 1960s (Table 7.17). For the non-naturalized, the modal decade was the 1970s.

While naturalized citizens had resided in the United States for much longer than the non-naturalized, there was little difference in the length of residence between those who had initiated naturalization and those who had not (Table 7.18).

Regardless of naturalization status, the modal age range at immigration was 19 to 30 years-of-age (Table 7.19).

More than 80 percent of the naturalized received their permanent resident visa prior to 1979 (Table 7.20). More than 40 percent of those who had not initiated naturalization, on the other hand, received their visa in 1979 or after.

Both the naturalized and the non-naturalized demonstrated a pattern of visiting their country of origin, but not more than once a year (Table 7.21).

Although overwhelming majorities of naturalized and non-naturalized Latino immigrants reported that they had close relatives living in the country of origin, the naturalized were slightly less likely to have relatives abroad (Table 7.22).

The naturalized, on the other hand, were slightly more likely to have relatives in the United States who did not live in their households (Table 7.23). Again, however, overwhelming majorities, regardless of citizenship status, had non-household-member relatives in the United States.

Questions Asked: F, G, H, K, L, 3, 6, 12, 14, 15, 16, 24, 25, 31, 33, 34, 58, 62a, 62b, 62c, 62d, 64, 64a, 68, 105, 106, and 107.
Tables with Comparable Data in Latino Voices: *Latino Voices* does not report data by naturalization status.

TABLE 7.2 Gender, by Stage in the Naturalization Process

Gender	*Not Initiated*	*Initiated, Not Completed*	*Naturalized Citizen*
Female	344 57.4%	241 53.3%	239 58.6%
Male	256 42.6%	212 46.7%	169 41.4%
Total	600 100.0%	453 100.0%	409 100.0%

Note: For country-of-origin data, see Table 3.1.

TABLE 7.3 Age, by Stage in the Naturalization Process

Age	Not Initiated	Initiated, Not Completed	Naturalized Citizen
18-24	77 12.8%	67 14.7%	26 6.3%
25-34	170 28.3%	124 27.4%	87 21.2%
35-50	207 34.6%	149 32.9%	169 41.3%
51-65	88 14.6%	70 15.5%	78 19.0%
66 or older	59 9.8%	43 9.5%	50 12.3%
Total	600 100.0%	453 100.0%	409 100.0%

Note: For country-of-origin data, see Table 3.2.

TABLE 7.4 Respondent's Education, by Stage in the Naturalization Process

Education	Not Initiated	Initiated, Not Completed	Naturalized Citizen
0-8 years	356 59.3%	170 37.5%	95 23.2%
9-12 years, no degree	68 11.3%	74 16.3%	80 19.5%
High school graduate	139 23.1%	146 32.2%	119 29.2%
Beyond high school	38 6.3%	64 14.0%	115 28.1%
Total	600 100.0%	453 100.0%	409 100.0%

Note: For country-of-origin data, see Table 3.11.

TABLE 7.5 Yearly Household Income, by Stage in the Naturalization Process

Household Income (1988)	*Not Initiated*	*Initiated, Not Completed*	*Naturalized Citizen*
Less than $6,000	62 10.3%	44 9.6%	19 4.6%
$6,000-$9,600	92 15.3%	74 16.3%	51 12.4%
$9,601-$14,400	102 17.0%	64 14.1%	27 6.6%
$14,401-$17,999	42 6.9%	38 8.4%	45 11.1%
$18,000-$24,000	99 16.5%	81 17.8%	80 19.5%
$24,001-$30,000	55 9.1%	66 14.5%	45 11.0%
$30,001-$36,000	28 4.7%	23 5.1%	45 11.1%
$36,001 or more	33 5.6%	19 4.2%	57 14.1%
Refused to answer	88 14.6%	46 10.1%	40 9.7%
Total	600 100.0%	453 100.0%	409 100.0%

Note: For country-of-origin data, see Table 3.17.

TABLE 7.6 Per Capita Household Income, by Stage in the Naturalization Process

Per Capita Household Income (1988)	*Not Initiated*	*Initiated, Not Completed*	*Naturalized Citizen*
$2,500 or less	57 9.9%	40 9.3%	14 3.7%
$2,501-$5,000	126 21.8%	93 21.9%	42 11.0%
$5,001-$10,000	159 27.6%	118 27.8%	140 36.1%
$10,001-$20,000	124 21.5%	103 24.3%	113 29.2%
$20,001 or more	22 3.9%	25 6.0%	38 9.8%
Refused to answer	88 15.2%	46 10.7%	40 10.2%
Total	576 100.0%	426 100.0%	387 100.0%

Note: For country-of-origin data, see Table 3.18.

TABLE 7.7 Current Labor Force Status, by Stage in the Naturalization Process

Current Labor Force Status	*Not Initiated*	*Initiated, Not Completed*	*Naturalized Citizen*
In labor force	328 54.7%	247 54.5%	251 61.4%
Temporarily unemployed	55 9.2%	60 13.3%	9 2.3%
Not in labor force	217 36.1%	146 32.2%	148 36.3%
Total	600 100.0%	453 100.0%	409 100.0%

Note: For country-of-origin data, see Table 3.25.

TABLE 7.8 Current Occupation, by Stage in the Naturalization Process

Current Occupation	*Not Initiated*	*Initiated, Not Completed*	*Naturalized Citizen*
Household labor	16 3.2%	12 3.3%	5 1.5%
Service	74 15.1%	66 18.4%	46 13.0%
Farm labor	37 7.6%	10 2.9%	7 2.1%
Laborer	61 12.4%	29 8.1%	24 6.7%
Transport	17 3.6%	18 5.1%	12 3.4%
Operative	150 30.7%	77 21.6%	66 18.5%
Craftsperson	54 11.0%	66 18.3%	26 7.2%
Clerical	43 8.8%	45 12.5%	62 17.4%
Sales	8 1.5%	6 1.6%	8 2.2%
Manager	19 3.8%	13 3.7%	28 7.7%
Professional	11 2.3%	16 4.4%	73 20.3%
Total	489 100.0%	358 100.0%	357 100.0%

Note: For country-of-origin data, see Table 3.27.

TABLE 7.9 Tenancy, by Stage in the Naturalization Process

Tenancy	*Not Initiated*	*Initiated, Not Completed*	*Naturalized Citizen*
Own	274 45.8%	212 47.0%	255 62.6%
Rent	308 51.5%	220 48.6%	145 35.5%
Other living arrangements	17 2.8%	20 4.4%	8 1.9%
Total	599 100.0%	452 100.0%	408 100.0%

Note: For country-of-origin data, see Table 3.36.

TABLE 7.10 Length of Residence in Same Area, by Stage in Naturalization Process

Residence in Same Area (years)	*Not Initiated*	*Initiated, Not Completed*	*Naturalized Citizen*
5 or fewer	141 24.6%	139 32.1%	63 15.7%
6-10	186 32.3%	116 26.7%	100 24.9%
11-20	189 32.9%	137 31.7%	131 32.5%
21 or more	59 10.2%	41 9.5%	108 26.9%
Total	574 100.0%	433 100.0%	401 100.0%

Note: For country-of-origin data, see Table 3.38.

TABLE 7.11 Language Spoken at Home, by Stage in the Naturalization Process

Language Usually Spoken at Home	*Not Initiated*	*Initiated, Not Completed*	*Naturalized Citizen*
English	31 5.1%	57 12.6%	52 12.7%
Spanish	481 80.1%	304 67.1%	247 60.4%
Both English and Spanish	89 14.8%	92 20.3%	110 26.9%
Total	600 100.0%	453 100.0%	409 100.0%

Note: For country-of-origin data, see Table 3.39.

TABLE 7.12 Self-Evaluated English Speaking Ability, by Stage in the Naturalization Process

English Speaking Ability	*Not Initiated*	*Initiated, Not Completed*	*Naturalized Citizen*
Very well	69 11.4%	85 18.9%	135 33.1%
Well	80 13.4%	105 23.2%	116 28.5%
Not well	265 44.2%	172 37.9%	131 32.1%
Not at all	186 31.0%	91 20.0%	26 6.3%
Total	600 100.0%	453 100.0%	409 100.0%

Note: For country-of-origin data, see Table 3.40.

TABLE 7.13 Self-Evaluated English Listening Comprehension, by Stage in the Naturalization Process

English Listening Comprehension Ability	*Not Initiated*	*Initiated, Not Completed*	*Naturalized Citizen*
Very well	102 17.0%	127 28.0%	170 41.5%
Well	99 16.4%	112 24.6%	112 27.4%
Not well	291 48.4%	166 36.6%	118 28.8%
Not at all	109 18.1%	49 10.8%	9 2.2%
Total	600 100.0%	453 100.0%	409 100.0%

Note: For country-of-origin data, see Table 3.41.

TABLE 7.14 Self-Evaluated English Writing Ability, by Stage in the Naturalization Process

English Writing Ability	*Not Initiated*	*Initiated, Not Completed*	*Naturalized Citizen*
Very well	64 10.7%	90 19.9%	155 37.9%
Well	64 10.7%	82 18.1%	77 18.9%
Not well	185 30.8%	133 29.4%	124 30.3%
Not at all	287 47.8%	148 32.6%	53 12.9%
Total	600 100.0%	453 100.0%	409 100.0%

Note: For country-of-origin data, see Table 3.42.

TABLE 7.15 Self-Evaluated English Reading Ability, by Stage in the Naturalization Process

English Reading Ability	*Not Initiated*	*Initiated, Not Completed*	*Naturalized Citizen*
Very well	75 12.5%	121 26.7%	177 43.4%
Well	87 14.4%	92 20.3%	102 24.9%
Not well	226 37.7%	147 32.4%	113 27.7%
Not at all	213 35.5%	93 20.6%	17 4.0%
Total	600 100.0%	453 100.0%	409 100.0%

Note: For country-of-origin data, see Table 3.43.

TABLE 7.16 Study of English in the United States, by Stage in the Naturalization Process

Study of English Since Immigration	*Not Initiated*	*Initiated, Not Completed*	*Naturalized Citizen*
Yes	281 46.8%	348 76.7%	329 80.6%
No	319 53.2%	106 23.3%	79 19.4%
Total	600 100.0%	453 100.0%	409 100.0%

Note: For country-of-origin data, see Table 3.46.

TABLE 7.17 Decade of Immigration, by Stage in the Naturalization Process

Decade of Immigration to Permanent Residence	*Not Initiated*	*Initiated, Not Completed*	*Naturalized Citizen*
1950s or before	45 8.1%	36 8.8%	88 22.4%
1960s	152 27.6%	117 29.0%	205 52.1%
1970s	308 55.9%	211 52.6%	91 23.1%
1980s	46 8.4%	39 9.6%	9 2.3%
Total	551 100.0%	402 100.0%	392 100.0%

Note: For country-of-origin data, see Table 3.48.

TABLE 7.18 Length of U.S. Residence, by Stage in the Naturalization Process

Length of U.S. Residence (years)	*Not Initiated*	*Initiated, Not Completed*	*Naturalized Citizen*
10 or fewer	178 32.3%	132 32.8%	34 8.7%
11-15	126 22.8%	81 20.2%	38 9.8%
16-20	135 24.4%	101 25.1%	94 24.0%
21-30	82 14.9%	62 15.5%	166 42.4%
31 or more	30 5.5%	26 6.5%	59 15.1%
Total	551 100.0%	402 100.0%	392 100.0%

Note: For country-of-origin data, see Table 3.49.

TABLE 7.19 Age at Immigration, by Stage in the Naturalization Process

Age at Immigration	*Not Initiated*	*Initiated, Not Completed*	*Naturalized Citizen*
6 or younger	43 7.2%	32 7.0%	50 12.4%
7-18	150 25.1%	148 32.8%	125 31.0%
19-30	251 42.2%	149 33.1%	140 34.9%
31 or older	152 25.5%	122 27.0%	87 21.8%
Total	597 100.0%	451 100.0%	402 100.0%

Note: For country-of-origin data, see Table 3.50.

TABLE 7.20 Year Received Permanent Resident (Legal Immigrant) Visa, by Stage in the Naturalization Process

Year Received Permanent Resident Visa	*Not Initiated*	*Initiated, Not Completed*	*Naturalized Citizen*
1965 or before	88 15.2%	72 16.2%	154 41.5%
1966-1978	254 43.8%	203 46.1%	178 48.0%
1979-1988	237 41.0%	167 37.7%	39 10.5%
Total	579 100.0%	441 100.0%	371 100.0%

Note: For country-of-origin data, see Table 3.53.

TABLE 7.21 Number of Visits to Home Country Per Year, by Stage in the Naturalization Process

Visits to Home Country Per Year of Residence	*Not Initiated*	*Initiated, Not Completed*	*Naturalized Citizen*
No visits	244 42.2%	163 38.8%	170 43.0%
One visit per year or less	270 46.7%	203 48.4%	187 47.2%
More than one and less than three visits per year	30 5.1%	28 6.7%	22 5.6%
Three or more visits per year	34 5.9%	25 6.0%	17 4.2%
Total	578 100.0%	419 100.0%	397 100.0%

Note: For country-of-origin data, see Table 3.59.

TABLE 7.22 Close Relatives Living in Home Country, by Stage in the Naturalization Process

Close Relatives Living in Home Country	*Not Initiated*	*Initiated, Not Completed*	*Naturalized Citizen*
Yes	560 93.3%	424 93.5%	340 83.2%
No	40 6.7%	29 6.5%	69 16.8%
Total	600 100.0%	453 100.0%	408 100.0%

Note: For country-of-origin data, see Table 3.64.

TABLE 7.23 Close Relatives Living in the United States, but Outside Household, by Stage in the Naturalization Process

Close Relatives Living in the United States, but Outside Household	*Not Initiated*	*Initiated, Not Completed*	*Naturalized Citizen*
Yes	506 84.5%	373 82.3%	368 90.0%
No	93 15.5%	80 17.7%	41 10.0%
Total	599 100.0%	453 100.0%	409 100.0%

Note: For country-of-origin data, see Table 3.65.

Organizational Behavior, Perceptions of Discrimination, and Political Activities

Findings

Few Latino immigrants were members of community organizations, with the exception of churches (Table 7.24). Although their numbers were small, the naturalized were more likely than the non-naturalized to be organizational members.

While the small numbers of Latino immigrants active in community organizations limit the level of confidence in this finding, it appears that the naturalized were less likely than the non-naturalized to be involved in organizations in which the majority of the members were Latino (Table 7.25).

Slight majorities of Latino immigrants, regardless of immigrant status, believed that U.S. society discriminates against Latinos (Table 7.26).

Despite this generalized feeling about discrimination against Latinos, between 18 and 26 percent reported that their families had experienced discrimination (Table 7.27). The naturalized were the most likely to report that their families had experienced discrimination.

Among those who reported having experienced discrimination, few reported that they experienced it frequently (Table 7.28). The majority of the non-naturalized reported experiencing discrimination rarely.

Small numbers believed that the INS discriminates against Latinos (Table 7.29). The group most likely to believe that INS discriminates was those who had begun but not yet completed naturalization.

Among Latino immigrants who resided as adults in their country of origin, the most common political activity was participating in a political march (Table 7.30). Regardless of naturalization status, less than half had participated in home-country politics. The most likely to have participated were those who had begun but not yet completed naturalization.

Naturalized citizens were more likely than the non-naturalized to follow U.S. politics in the news (Table 7.31). Regardless of naturalization status, however, the majority reported that they followed U.S. politics in the news.

Questions Asked: L, 46, 47, 48, 48a, 54, 55, 56, 64, 64a, 68, and 100.
Tables with Comparable Data in Latino Voices: *Latino Voices* does not report data by naturalization status.

TABLE 7.24 Membership in Community Organizations, by Stage in the Naturalization Process

Type of Organization	*Not Initiated*	*Initiated, Not Completed*	*Naturalized Citizen*
Church	328 54.6% (n=600)	274 60.5% (n=453)	282 69.0% (n=409)
PTA	109 18.2% (n=600)	98 21.6% (n=453)	133 32.5% (n=409)
Sports club	53 8.9% (n=600)	80 17.7% (n=453)	69 17.0% (n=409)
Social club	49 8.1% (n=600)	51 11.2% (n=453)	63 15.4% (n=409)
National-origin club	49 8.1% (n=600)	48 10.6% (n=453)	50 12.2% (n=409)
Union	43 7.2% (n=600)	37 8.3% (n=449)	61 15.0% (n=409)
Political club	5 0.8% (n=600)	24 5.2% (n=453)	24 6.0% (n=409)
Fraternal club	11 1.8% (n=600)	17 3.7% (n=453)	31 7.5% (n=409)
Senior citizens club	9 1.4% (n=600)	9 1.9% (n=453)	16 3.8% (n=409)

Note: For country-of-origin data, see Table 4.8.

TABLE 7.25 Latinos in Organizations to Which Respondent Belonged, by Stage in the Naturalization Process

Type of Organization	*Not Initiated*	*Initiated, Not Completed*	*Naturalized Citizen*
Majority Latino church	273 83.7% (n=327)	232 85.1% (n=272)	182 65.3% (n=280)
Majority Latino PTA	63 58.1% (n=108)	47 48.5% (n=96)	43 32.3% (n=132)
Majority Latino sports club	31 57.3% (n=53)	50 62.8% (n=79)	37 53.6% (n=69)
Majority Latino social club	38 78.2% (n=49)	25 48.7% (n=51)	36 58.4% (n=62)
Majority Latino nationality club	48 98.6% (n=49)	46 96.2% (n=48)	49 97.7% (n=50)
Majority Latino union	14 33.4% (n=42)	17 45.4% (n=37)	19 32.1% (n=59)
Majority Latino political club	5 100.0% (n=5)	20 84.9% (n=24)	10 41.6% (n=23)
Majority Latino fraternal club	9 95.7% (n=9)	8 47.8% (n=17)	15 50.6% (n=29)
Majority Latino seniors club	6 74.6% (n=9)	6 70.1% (n=9)	4 27.2% (n=15)

Note: For country-of-origin data, see Table 4.9.

TABLE 7.26 Perception of Discrimination Against Latinos, by Stage in the Naturalization Process

Does U.S. Society Discriminate Against Latinos?	*Not Initiated*	*Initiated, Not Completed*	*Naturalized Citizen*
Yes	303 53.7%	247 56.9%	192 50.2%
No	240 42.5%	173 39.9%	181 47.3%
Unsure	21 3.8%	14 3.3%	10 2.5%
Total	565 100.0%	434 100.0%	384 100.0%

Note: For country-of-origin data, see Table 5.1.

TABLE 7.27 Personal or Familial Experience of Discrimination, by Stage in the Naturalization Process

Has Respondent's Family Experienced Discrimination?	*Not Initiated*	*Initiated, Not Completed*	*Naturalized Citizen*
Yes	106 17.7%	87 19.3%	104 25.6%
No	492 82.3%	362 80.7%	302 74.4%
Total	598 100.0%	448 100.0%	406 100.0%

Note: For country-of-origin data, see Table 5.2

TABLE 7.28 Frequency of Familial Discrimination, by Stage in the Naturalization Process

Frequency of Familial Discrimination	*Not Initiated*	*Initiated, Not Completed*	*Naturalized Citizen*
Rarely	55 51.6%	49 56.2%	41 40.7%
Occasionally	33 31.3%	29 33.6%	41 40.4%
Frequently	18 17.1%	9 10.2%	19 18.8%
Total	106 100.0%	87 100.0%	101 100.0%

Note: For country-of-origin data, see Table 5.3.

TABLE 7.29 Perception of INS Discrimination Against Latinos, by Stage in the Naturalization Process

Does INS Discriminate Against Latinos More Than Other Immigrant Ethnic Groups?	*Not Initiated*	*Initiated, Not Completed*	*Naturalized Citizen*
Yes	119 20.3%	152 33.9%	110 27.2%
No	302 51.2%	194 43.2%	195 48.3%
Unsure	168 28.5%	103 22.9%	99 24.5%
Total	589 100.0%	449 100.0%	403 100.0%

Note: For country-of-origin data, see Table 5.4.

TABLE 7.30 Participation in Home-Country Political Activity, Among Respondents Who Migrated as Adults, by Stage in the Naturalization Process

Type of Home-Country Political Activity	*Not Initiated*	*Initiated, Not Completed*	*Naturalized Citizen*
Followed political news	157 35.8% (n=440)	130 44.6% (n=292)	72 30.1% (n=240)
Marched	199 45.4% (n=438)	121 41.4% (n=292)	102 41.6% (n=239)
Voted	26 5.9% (n=440)	35 12.0% (n=291)	11 4.7% (n=242)

Note: For country-of-origin data, see Table 5.9.

TABLE 7.31 Participation in U.S. Political Activity, by Stage in the Naturalization Process

Type of U.S. Political Activity	*Not Initiated*	*Initiated, Not Completed*	*Naturalized Citizen*
Followed political news	308 51.8% (n=596)	261 58.2% (n=448)	276 67.8% (n=407)
Wrote letters about U.S. political issues	21 3.5% (n=595)	46 10.3% (n=451)	58 14.3% (n=406)
Distributed leaflets about political issues	7 1.2% (n=591)	31 6.8% (n=451)	43 10.7% (n=406)
Marched	21 3.5% (n=593)	40 9.0% (n=447)	63 15.6% (n=407)
Contributed money or attended fundraisers	15 2.7% (n=551)	56 13.2% (n=426)	301 74.0% (n=407)
Voted	21 3.6% (n=588)	49 10.9% (n=449)	80 19.5% (n=408)
Helped people register to vote	8 1.4% (n=592)	27 6.0% (n=447)	15 3.7% (n=408)

Note: For country-of-origin data, see Table 5.10.

Attachment to the United States and Attitudes Toward and Experiences with Naturalization

Findings

Regardless of whether Latino immigrants had naturalized or, among the non-naturalized, whether they had begun to naturalize, almost all planned to make the United States their permanent home (Table 7.32).

A small share—between 8 and 15 percent—believed that life was better in the country of origin (Table 7.33). Interestingly, naturalized citizens were the most likely to believe this.

As would be expected, the majority of the non-naturalized identified more with the home country than with the United States and the majority of the naturalized identified more with the United States than with the home country (Table 7.34). Interestingly, a significant component of the non-naturalized identified more with the United States and many of the naturalized identified more with the home country.

Almost universally, Latino immigrants anticipated that their children's lives would be better than their own (Table 7.35). This attitude was particularly strong among the non-naturalized.

The majority of respondents—including those who had not yet initiated naturalization—believed that becoming a U.S. citizen was "very important" (Table 7.36). Few believed the converse—that it was "not at all important."

Among those who had not yet naturalized, there was strong support among their peers for naturalization (Table 7.37).

Among the naturalized and those who had initiated but not completed naturalization, access to the vote was the reason for naturalizing most likely to be seen as "very important" (Table 7.38).

When asked to provide the single most important reason for naturalizing, both the naturalized and non-naturalized indicated that naturalization allowed for more complete participation in American life (Table 7.39).

When given a series of reasons for not naturalizing, respondents who had initiated naturalization were most likely to indicate as a "very important" reason the perception that there were no benefits in naturalizing (Table 7.40). Among those who had not initiated naturalization, the difficulty of the citizenship exam and the perception that there were no benefits in naturalizing were virtually tied. Neither of these explanations, however, was very important to a majority of respondents. The most important single reason for not naturalizing was simply not having considered it (Table 7.41).

The majority of those who had not begun to naturalize had not taken English classes (Table 7.42). Among those who had initiated but not completed the naturalization process, the majority had taken English classes, but not necessarily with the intent of preparing for naturalization.

The majority of the naturalized and those in the process of naturalizing had taken history and civics classes (Table 7.43). Among those in the process who had taken classes, the majority had undertaken these studies specifically to prepare for the naturalization exam (Table 7.44).

The naturalized had begun to seek naturalization well before those who were still in the process (Table 7.45). Among those who had initiated but not completed naturalization, almost four in five began the process in the 1980s.

As would be expected, Latino immigrants who had failed the naturalization exam were more likely than those who had passed to report that it was "very" or "somewhat" hard (Table 7.46). Even though they had failed, however, the majority of these respondents reported that the exam was "somewhat" or "very" easy.

Questions Asked: L, 10, 42, 52, 53, 64, 64a, 65, 68, 70, 84c, 91, 92a, 97, 98, and 102.
Tables with Comparable Data in Latino Voices: *Latino Voices* does not report data by naturalization status.

TABLE 7.32 Plans to Make a Permanent Home of the United States, by Stage in the Naturalization Process

Plans to Make a Permanent Home of the United States	*Not Initiated*	*Initiated, Not Completed*	*Naturalized Citizen*
Yes	569 97.2%	438 97.6%	403 99.1%
No	16 2.8%	11 2.4%	4 0.9%
Total	585 100.0%	449 100.0%	406 100.0%

Note: For country-of-origin data, see Table 6.1.

TABLE 7.33 Evaluation of Where Life is Better, by Stage in the Naturalization Process

Where Life is Better	*Not Initiated*	*Initiated, Not Completed*	*Naturalized Citizen*
In the United States	459 79.2%	360 81.0%	300 75.1%
In country of origin	62 10.7%	33 7.5%	61 15.4%
In another place	58 10.0%	51 11.5%	38 9.6%
Total	579 100.0%	445 100.0%	399 100.0%

Note: For country-of-origin data, see Table 6.2.

TABLE 7.34 National Self-Identification, by Stage in the Naturalization Process

National Self-Identification	*Not Initiated*	*Initiated, Not Completed*	*Naturalized Citizen*
With the United States	184 32.0%	169 38.7%	204 50.5%
With the country of origin	358 62.2%	246 56.2%	153 37.9%
With some other country	34 5.8%	22 5.1%	47 11.6%
Total	576 100.0%	438 100.0%	403 100.0%

Note: For country-of-origin data, see Table 6.3.

TABLE 7.35 Anticipations for Children's Lifestyle, by Stage in the Naturalization Process

Expected Lifestyle of Children	*Not Initiated*	*Initiated, Not Completed*	*Naturalized Citizen*
Better than respondent	377 90.6%	301 93.9%	255 87.3%
Same as respondent	33 7.9%	17 5.2%	21 7.3%
Worse than respondent	6 1.5%	3 1.0%	16 5.4%
Total	416 100.0%	321 100.0%	292 100.0%

Note: For country-of-origin data, see Table 6.4.

TABLE 7.36 Importance of Becoming a U.S. Citizen, by Stage in the Naturalization Process

Importance of Becoming a U.S. Citizen	*Not Initiated*	*Initiated, Not Completed*	*Naturalized Citizen*
Very	306 52.2%	309 69.1%	346 84.8%
Somewhat	165 28.1%	98 21.9%	41 9.9%
Not very	78 13.4%	36 8.0%	8 2.0%
Not at all	37 6.4%	5 1.0%	13 3.3%
Total	586 100.0%	447 100.0%	408 100.0%

Note: For country-of-origin data, see Table 6.5.

TABLE 7.37 Peers' Attitudes Toward Respondent Naturalizing, Among Those Non-citizens Who Had Discussed Naturalization, by Stage in the Naturalization Process

Peers' Attitudes Toward Respondent Naturalizing	*Not Initiated*	*Initiated, Not Completed*
Favor	193 90.6%	224 85.9%
Oppose	6 2.8%	24 9.2%
Mixed views	14 6.7%	13 4.9%
Total	213 100.0%	261 100.0%

Note: For country-of-origin data, see Table 6.7.

TABLE 7.38 Reasons for Seeking U.S. Citizenship, by Stage in the Naturalization Process

Reason (Ranked as Very Important)	*Not Initiated*	*Initiated, Not Completed*	*Naturalized Citizen*
Naturalization allows the vote	484 82.7% (n=585)	399 89.3% (n=447)	393 96.2% (n=408)
Naturalization increases opportunities for children	471 80.8% (n=583)	381 85.7% (n=445)	290 71.6% (n=406)
Naturalization helps relatives immigrate	460 78.0% (n=589)	370 82.3% (n=449)	289 71.7% (n=403)
Naturalization offers additional legal protections	439 75.1% (n=584)	356 80.2% (n=444)	289 71.4% (n=405)

(continues)

TABLE 7.38 *(continued)*

Reason (Ranked as Very Important)	*Not Initiated*	*Initiated, Not Completed*	*Naturalized Citizen*
Naturalization gives children citizenship	427 72.1% (n=592)	337 74.7% (n=451)	290 72.7% (n=399)
Naturalization expands job opportunities	441 74.2% (n=594)	340 75.3% (n=451)	250 63.4% (n=395)
Naturalization establishes eligibility for government programs	413 70.0% (n=591)	327 73.4% (n=445)	277 68.0% (n=407)
Naturalization allows equal participation in American life	391 66.9% (n=584)	334 74.1% (n=451)	286 70.7% (n=404)
Naturalization improves life in general	380 64.5% (n=590)	317 70.7% (n=447)	267 67.2% (n=397)
Naturalization increases opportunities to earn money	346 59.2% (n=585)	279 62.2% (n=448)	188 48.4% (n=389)

Note: For country-of-origin data, see Table 6.11.

TABLE 7.39 Most Important Reason for Naturalizing, by Stage in the Naturalization Process

Most Important Reason for Naturalizing	*Not Initiated*	*Initiated, Not Completed*	*Naturalized Citizen*
To participate more fully in American life	145 24.2%	121 26.8%	146 35.8%
To participate in American politics	89 14.8%	75 16.4%	69 16.8%
To express gratitude to the United States	33 5.4%	49 10.7%	56 13.7%
To attain eligibility for specific benefits	90 15.0%	65 14.4%	39 9.5%
To achieve economic opportunities	52 8.6%	33 7.3%	33 8.2%
To help children	14 2.3%	11 2.5%	3 0.8%
To assure a better life	52 8.6%	24 5.4%	20 4.9%
To resolve own or family's immigration problems	18 3.0%	19 4.1%	13 3.1%
To reduce discrimination	2 0.4%	3 0.7%	4 1.0%
There is no reason to naturalize	41 6.8%	5 1.2%	8 2.1%
No opinion	64 10.7%	48 10.5%	17 4.2%
Total	600 100.0%	453 100.0%	409 100.0%

Note: For country-of-origin data, see Table 6.12.

TABLE 7.40 Reasons for Not Seeking U.S. Citizenship Among Those Who Have Not Naturalized, by Stage in the Naturalization Process

Reason (Ranked as Very Important)	*Not Initiated*	*Initiated, Not Completed*
Perception that there are no benefits in naturalization	160 28.0% (n=572)	132 32.9% (n=402)
Difficulty of U.S. citizenship exam	165 28.2% (n=584)	71 17.6% (n=406)
Latinos face discrimination in the United States	102 17.9% (n=570)	87 21.1% (n=414)
Desire to keep land in home country	107 18.3% (n=585)	52 12.8% (n=409)
Feelings of disloyalty to home country	88 15.5% (n=569)	51 12.1% (n=419)
Maintenance of political ties with country of origin	79 13.6% (n=586)	52 12.6% (n=416)
Fear of loss of culture	61 10.4% (n=587)	59 14.1% (n=416)
Fear of INS mistreatment	51 8.8% (n=574)	34 8.3% (n=409)
Plan to live permanently in home country	53 9.2% (n=576)	29 7.1% (n=413)

Note: For country-of-origin data, see Table 6.14.

TABLE 7.41 Most Important Reason for Not Seeking Naturalization, Among Non-U.S.-Citizens, by Stage in the Naturalization Process

Most Important Reason for Not Naturalizing	*Not Initiated*	*Initiated,Not Completed*
Has not considered	219 39.8%	132 44.7%
Love of home country	63 11.4%	50 16.8%
No reason to naturalize	73 13.2%	29 9.8%
Does not speak English	68 12.4%	31 10.5%
Intends to return to country of origin	47 8.5%	11 3.6%
Believes that it is not possible to naturalize	46 8.4%	18 6.2%
Desires to maintain property in home country	22 3.9%	17 5.6%
Other	13 2.4%	8 2.8%
Total	551 100.0%	296 100.0%

Note: For country-of-origin data, see Table 6.15.

TABLE 7.42 Study of English to Prepare for Naturalization, by Stage in the Naturalization Process

English Study to Prepare for Naturalization	*Not Initiated*	*Initiated, Not Completed*	*Naturalized Citizen*
Has not taken English classes	319 53.2%	106 23.3%	79 19.4%
Has taken English classes, but not to prepare for citizenship	281 46.8%	194 42.8%	249 61.0%
Has taken English classes to prepare for U.S. citizenship	0 0.0%	154 33.9%	80 19.6%
Total	600 100.0%	453 100.0%	409 100.0%

Note: For country-of-origin data, see Table 6.16.

TABLE 7.43 Study of U.S. History and Civics, by Stage in the Naturalization Process

U.S. History and Civics Study	*Not Initiated*	*Initiated, Not Completed*	*Naturalized Citizen*
Yes	119 19.8%	261 57.6%	323 79.5%
No	481 80.2%	192 42.4%	84 20.5%
Total	600 100.0%	453 100.0%	407 100.0%

Note: For country-of-origin data, see Table 6.17.

TABLE 7.44 Study of U.S. History and Civics to Prepare for Naturalization, by Stage in the Naturalization Process

U.S. History and Civics Study to Prepare for Naturalization	*Not Initiated*	*Initiated, Not Completed*	*Naturalized Citizen*
Yes	0 0.0%	163 36.0%	150 36.8%
No	119 19.8%	98 21.5%	173 42.2%
Has not taken history or civics classes	481 80.2%	193 42.5%	86 20.9%
Total	600 100.0%	453 100.0%	409 100.0%

Note: For country-of-origin data, see Table 6.18.

TABLE 7.45 Decade in Which Applicants Began Application Process, by Stage in the Naturalization Process

Decade in Which Respondent Obtained the Application	*Initiated, Not Completed*	*Naturalized Citizen*
1960s or before	19 6.4%	79 20.9%
1970s	42 14.3%	138 36.5%
1980s	234 79.4%	162 42.6%
Total	295 100.0%	379 100.0%

Note: For country-of-origin data, see Table 6.26.

TABLE 7.46 Difficulty of the Citizenship Exam, by Stage in the Naturalization Process

Difficulty of the Citizenship Exam	*Initiated, Not Completed*	*Naturalized Citizen*
Very hard	8 19.4%	26 7.5%
Somewhat hard	8 19.0%	45 13.1%
Somewhat easy	7 17.9%	102 29.3%
Very easy	18 43.8%	174 50.2%
Total	42 100.0%	347 100.0%

Note: For country-of-origin data, see Table 6.38.

8

Selected Latino Immigrant Characteristics for High-Concentration States

Immigration in general, and Latino immigration specifically, does not result in an even distribution of immigrants across the country. Instead, immigrants tend to concentrate in certain regions of the country. With turn-of-the-century immigrants, these areas of concentration included port cities in the Northeast, Chicago, and San Francisco. Today, the ports of entry include some U.S. cities near the U.S.-Mexico border, such as Los Angeles and Houston, and cities with major international air links to other countries such as Miami, New York, San Francisco, and, again, Los Angeles. Each of these cities and the states of California, Florida, New York, and Texas have received large numbers of Latino and non-Latino immigrants over the past twenty years.

Just as New York at the turn of the century received immigrants from throughout Europe, today California, Florida, New York, and Texas are the destinations of people from many different countries. This pattern of immigrants of different nationalities locating in a single area applies to Latinos as well. Los Angeles and Southern California, for example, were traditional destinations for Mexican immigrants. Today, Mexican immigrants are not the only Latin American immigrants in Los Angeles. They are joined by large numbers of Guatemalans, Salvadorans, and others from Central and South America. Miami and South Florida, which were traditionally the locus for immigrants from the Caribbean, today receive immigrants from Central and South America as well. These patterns repeat themselves in each of the major immigrant ports of entry.

In an effort to examine immigrants in a regional rather than national origin context, in this chapter we focus on immigrants in the four states with the largest share of Latino immigrants eligible for naturalization. Among Latino immigrants in California, Florida, New York, and Texas, we examine social and demographic characteristics; organizational and political activities and perceptions; attachment to the United States; and attitudes towards and experiences with naturalization. More than four in five Latino immigrants resided in these four states at the time of the survey. While the concentrations of the various Latino nationality groups varied in each of the states, none exclusively contained immigrants of one Latino nationality. The relative concentrations varied. Texas had the highest concentration, with approximately 85 percent of the survey respondents coming from Mexico. In California, 74 percent of the NLIS respondents were born in Mexico. Among respondents in Florida, approximately 78 percent came from Cuba. Remembering that the NLIS excludes Puerto Ricans, New York sees a greater diversity of Latino immigrants groups. Thirty-six percent of NLIS respondents came from South American countries and 31 percent came from the Dominican Republic. In California and Texas, the second most common region of origin was Central America and Cuba, respectively, with 13 and 8 percent of the states' respondents. In Florida, the second largest bloc of Latino immigrants was from South America. In this chapter, then, we examine commonalities and differences in the Latino immigrant experiences in the four states with the largest populations of Latino immigrants.

Social and Demographic Characteristics of Immigrants

Findings

Latino immigrants in New York were slightly more likely to be women, compared to those in the other states with large Latino immigrant populations (Table 8.1).

Latino immigrants in Texas had a larger share of their population in the younger age categories than those in California, Florida, or New York (Table 8.2). The modal age range for Latino immigrants, regardless of state, was thirty-five to fifty.

More than half of Latino immigrants in Texas had eight or fewer years of education (Table 8.3). At the other extreme, 46 percent of Latino immigrants in Florida had high school degrees or education beyond high school.

Latino immigrant household incomes varied by state (Table 8.4). More than one in ten Latino immigrants in California and Florida had incomes (in 1988) exceeding $36,000 per year whereas less than 4 percent of Latino immigrant households exceeded this income level. Moreover, in New York and Texas, 12 and 16 percent, respectively, had household incomes of less than $6,000. These variations between states also appear when we examine per capita income (Table 8.5).

Latino immigrants in Texas faced the highest levels of temporary unemployment (Table 8.6). Regardless of state, between 50 and 60 percent of Latino immigrants were in the work force at the time of the survey.

In all states but Florida, the most common occupational category was operative (Table 8.7). In Florida, service occupations were slightly more common than operatives and clerical employees.

With the exception of New York respondents, more than half of Latino immigrants owned their home (Table 8.8). In New York, one-quarter owned and more than two-thirds rented their home, following the pattern of higher-than-average levels of rentals among New York residents as a whole.

California and Florida Latino immigrants demonstrated more residential stability than their counterparts in New York and Texas (Table 8.9). The modal length of residence in the same area was eleven to twenty years for California and Florida respondents, one to five years for New York respondents, and six to ten years for Texas respondents.

Regardless of state, the majority of Latino immigrants spoke predominantly Spanish at home (Table 8.10). The highest levels of English and mixed English and Spanish use appeared in California.

Regardless of state, the modal self-reported level of English speaking ability was "not well" (Table 8.11). California and Florida respondents were the most likely to report that they spoke English "very well."

The majority of California, Florida, and New York respondents reported that they understood English either "very well" or "well" (Table 8.12). Conversely, just 36 percent of Texan respondents reported comparable levels of English listening ability.

Regardless of state, the majority of Latino immigrants reported that they wrote English either "not well" or "not at all" (Table 8.13). Although slightly more respondents reported that they could read English either "very well" or "well" than could write English at comparable levels, the majority reported their reading skills to be "not well" or "not at all" (Table 8.14).

Levels of post-immigration English-language study varied by state (Table 8.15). Seventy-five percent of Latino immigrants in California had taken classes compared to 56 percent in Texas.

California and Florida Latino immigrants were more likely to have migrated in the 1960s or before than were New York and Texas immigrants (Table 8.16). More than half of the Latino immigrants in these latter two states immigrated in the 1970s. The modal length of residence in the United States was twenty-one to thirty years among California and Florida Latino immigrants and less than ten years among New York and Texas immigrants (Table 8.17).

California and Texas Latino immigrants were the most likely to be children when they immigrated to the United States (Table 8.18). Forty-one percent and 48 percent, respectively, were eighteen-years-of-age or less. Latino immigrants in Florida were the most likely to have been thirty-one or older at the time of immigration.

Regardless of state, Latino immigrants were most likely to have received their permanent resident visas between 1966 and 1978 (Table 8.19). New Yorkers were the least likely to have received immigrant visas in 1965 or before and Californians and Floridians the least likely in 1979 or after.

Reflecting the nature of the relationship between Cuba and the United States, Latino immigrants in Florida were the least likely to have visited their country of origin (Table 8.20). Based on visits per year of residence, Latino immigrants in Texas were the most likely to make home-country visits.

Regardless of state, most Latino immigrants had close relatives living in the country of origin (Table 8.21). Most, though slightly fewer, also had close relatives living outside the household in the United States (Table 8.22).

Questions Asked: F, G, H, K, 3, 6, 12, 14, 15, 16, 24, 25, 31, 33, 34, 58, 62a, 62b, 62c, 62d, 64, 105, 106, and 107.
Tables with Comparable Data in Latino Voices: *Latino Voices* does not report data by state of residence.

TABLE 8.1 Gender, by State

Gender	*California*	*Florida*	*New York*	*Texas*
Female	249 57.5%	182 54.2%	168 59.9%	191 56.1%
Male	184 42.5%	153 45.8%	113 40.1%	149 43.9%
Total	432 100.0%	335 100.0%	281 100.0%	340 100.0%

Note: For country-of-origin data, see Table 3.1.

TABLE 8.2 Age, by State

Age	*California*	*Florida*	*New York*	*Texas*
18-24	47 10.8%	25 7.3%	20 7.1%	49 14.4%
25-34	127 29.4%	51 15.3%	68 24.3%	99 29.0%
35-50	154 35.7%	118 35.3%	125 44.7%	115 33.9%
51-65	70 16.1%	82 24.6%	39 13.8%	40 11.7%
66 or older	34 8.0%	59 17.5%	28 10.0%	37 11.0%
Total	432 100.0%	335 100.0%	281 100.0%	340 100.0%

Note: For country-of-origin data, see Table 3.2.

TABLE 8.3 Respondent's Education, by State

Education	*California*	*Florida*	*New York*	*Texas*
0-8 years	178 41.2%	93 27.7%	126 44.7%	201 59.2%
9-12 years, no degree	52 12.1%	87 25.8%	41 14.6%	32 9.4%
High school graduate	136 31.5%	87 26.0%	79 28.0%	85 24.9%
Beyond high school	66 15.2%	68 20.4%	36 12.7%	22 6.5%
Total	432 100.0%	335 100.0%	281 100.0%	340 100.0%

Note: For country-of-origin data, see Table 3.11.

TABLE 8.4 Yearly Household Income, by State

Household Income (1988)	*California*	*Florida*	*New York*	*Texas*
Less than $6,000	19 4.5%	24 7.2%	35 12.4%	53 15.7%
$6,000-$9,600	57 13.3%	54 16.1%	42 15.0%	60 17.5%
$9,601-$14,400	53 12.3%	33 9.9%	41 14.6%	60 17.5%
$14,401-$17,999	35 8.1%	26 7.6%	26 9.2%	24 7.2%
$18,000-$24,000	85 19.6%	68 20.3%	49 17.6%	40 11.8%
$24,001-$30,000	47 11.0%	40 11.9%	26 9.1%	45 13.2%
$30,001-$36,000	33 7.7%	17 5.1%	14 5.0%	10 2.8%
$36,001 or more	45 10.3%	38 11.3%	20 7.0%	12 3.5%
Refused to answer	57 13.2%	36 10.6%	28 9.9%	37 10.8%
Total	432 100.0%	335 100.0%	281 100.0%	340 100.0%

Note: For country-of-origin data, see Table 3.17.

TABLE 8.5 Per Capita Household Income, by State

Per Capita Household Income (1988)	*California*	*Florida*	*New York*	*Texas*
$2,500 or less	22 5.3%	18 5.8%	23 8.9%	53 16.2%
$2,501-$5,000	66 16.0%	58 18.4%	49 18.9%	81 24.8%
$5,001-$10,000	113 27.2%	108 34.3%	83 32.0%	70 21.3%
$10,001-$20,000	112 27.1%	74 23.4%	65 25.0%	79 24.2%
$20,001 or more	44 10.6%	22 6.8%	11 4.3%	7 2.1%
Refused to answer	57 13.8%	36 11.3%	28 10.8%	37 11.3%
Total	414 100.0%	315 100.0%	258 100.0%	326 100.0%

Note: For country-of-origin data, see Table 3.18.

TABLE 8.6 Current Labor Force Status, by State

Current Labor Force Status	*California*	*Florida*	*New York*	*Texas*
In labor force	253 58.6%	186 55.5%	151 53.9%	178 52.2%
Temporarily unemployed	32 7.3%	16 4.9%	24 8.4%	40 11.6%
Not in labor force	147 34.1%	133 39.7%	106 37.7%	123 36.2%
Total	432 100.0%	335 100.0%	281 100.0%	340 100.0%

Note: For country-of-origin data, see Table 3.25.

TABLE 8.7 Current Occupation, by State

Current Occupation	*California*	*Florida*	*New York*	*Texas*
Household labor	11 2.9%	1 0.4%	10 4.6%	13 4.9%
Service	54 14.6%	56 19.9%	37 16.4%	31 12.1%
Farm labor	40 10.8%	1 0.3%	0 0.0%	17 6.7%
Laborer	15 4.0%	13 4.7%	23 10.3%	44 17.1%
Transport	14 3.9%	6 2.3%	15 6.7%	6 2.5%
Operative	84 22.7%	53 18.8%	62 27.5%	73 28.5%
Craftsperson	45 12.1%	33 11.7%	18 8.1%	35 13.6%
Clerical	57 15.3%	53 18.8%	33 14.5%	16 6.4%
Sales	9 2.5%	10 3.5%	4 2.0%	0 0.1%
Manager	16 4.3%	25 8.7%	10 4.6%	10 3.8%
Professional	26 7.0%	31 10.8%	12 5.4%	11 4.2%
Total	372 100.0%	282 100.0%	224 100.0%	256 100.0%

Note: For country-of-origin data, see Table 3.27.

TABLE 8.8 Tenancy, by State

Tenancy	*California*	*Florida*	*New York*	*Texas*
Own	231 53.7%	200 60.0%	78 27.9%	196 57.6%
Rent	184 42.8%	129 38.5%	189 67.6%	130 38.2%
Other living arrangements	15 3.4%	5 1.6%	12 4.5%	14 4.2%
Total	431 100.0%	334 100.0%	279 100.0%	340 100.0%

Note: For country-of-origin data, see 3.36.

TABLE 8.9 Length of Residence in the Same Area, by State

Residence in Same Area (years)	*California*	*Florida*	*New York*	*Texas*
5 or fewer	96 23.1%	67 20.8%	92 34.5%	74 22.7%
6-10	100 23.9%	80 24.9%	83 31.3%	117 35.7%
11-20	133 31.8%	126 39.0%	71 26.5%	87 26.4%
21 or more	88 21.2%	49 15.3%	20 7.7%	50 15.2%
Total	417 100.0%	322 100.0%	266 100.0%	327 100.0%

Note: For country-of-origin data, see Table 3.38.

TABLE 8.10 Language Spoken at Home, by State

Language Usually Spoken at Home	*California*	*Florida*	*New York*	*Texas*
English	60 14.0%	18 5.5%	20 7.1%	35 10.3%
Spanish	284 65.7%	259 77.4%	198 70.6%	251 73.8%
Both English and Spanish	88 20.3%	57 17.1%	62 22.3%	54 15.9%
Total	432 100.0%	335 100.0%	281 100.0%	340 100.0%

Note: For country-of-origin data, see Table 3.39.

TABLE 8.11 Self-Evaluated English Speaking Ability, by State

English Speaking Ability	*California*	*Florida*	*New York*	*Texas*
Very well	91 21.1%	85 25.2%	42 15.1%	59 17.5%
Well	106 24.5%	63 18.9%	72 25.5%	44 12.9%
Not well	168 38.9%	117 35.1%	110 39.3%	144 42.4%
Not at all	67 15.5%	70 20.8%	56 20.1%	93 27.3%
Total	432 100.0%	335 100.0%	281 100.0%	340 100.0%

Note: For country-of-origin data, see Table 3.40.

TABLE 8.12 Self-Evaluated English Listening Comprehension, by State

English Listening Comprehension Ability	*California*	*Florida*	*New York*	*Texas*
Very well	125 28.9%	105 31.4%	65 23.1%	80 23.4%
Well	106 24.5%	71 21.1%	88 31.4%	44 12.9%
Not well	174 40.3%	111 33.3%	109 38.8%	153 45.0%
Not at all	28 6.4%	48 14.2%	19 6.7%	64 18.7%
Total	432 100.0%	335 100.0%	281 100.0%	340 100.0%

Note: For country-of-origin data, see Table 3.41.

TABLE 8.13 Self-Evaluated English Writing Ability, by State

English Writing Ability	*California*	*Florida*	*New York*	*Texas*
Very well	87 20.2%	93 27.7%	49 17.3%	61 17.8%
Well	89 20.6%	52 15.5%	51 18.3%	30 8.9%
Not well	124 28.7%	86 25.7%	99 35.3%	96 28.3%
Not at all	132 30.4%	104 31.1%	82 29.1%	153 45.0%
Total	432 100.0%	335 100.0%	281 100.0%	340 100.0%

Note: For country-of-origin data, see Table 3.42.

TABLE 8.14 Self-Evaluated English Reading Ability, by State

English Reading Ability	*California*	*Florida*	*New York*	*Texas*
Very well	108 25.1%	103 30.8%	71 25.3%	69 20.3%
Well	105 24.3%	67 19.9%	47 16.6%	48 14.1%
Not well	138 32.0%	107 31.8%	95 33.8%	115 33.9%
Not at all	80 18.5%	59 17.5%	68 24.3%	108 31.7%
Total	431 100.0%	335 100.0%	281 100.0%	340 100.0%

Note: For country-of-origin data, see Table 3.43.

TABLE 8.15 Study of English in the United States, by State

Study of English Since Immigration	*California*	*Florida*	*New York*	*Texas*
Yes	324 74.9%	227 67.8%	169 60.2%	189 55.5%
No	108 25.1%	108 32.2%	112 39.8%	151 44.5%
Total	432 100.0%	335 100.0%	281 100.0%	340 100.0%

Note: For country-of-origin data, see Table 3.46.

TABLE 8.16 Decade of Immigration, by State

Decade of Immigration to Permanent Residence	*California*	*Florida*	*New York*	*Texas*
1950s or before	74 17.8%	47 15.3%	16 6.5%	45 14.8%
1960s	137 33.0%	147 47.6%	81 32.6%	63 20.9%
1970s	169 40.7%	102 33.0%	142 57.1%	165 55.0%
1980s	35 8.4%	12 4.0%	9 3.8%	28 9.2%
Total	415 100.0%	308 100.0%	248 100.0%	300 100.0%

Note: For country-of-origin data, see Table 3.48.

TABLE 8.17 Length of U.S. Residence, by State

Length of U.S. Residence (years)	*California*	*Florida*	*New York*	*Texas*
10 or fewer	95 22.8%	67 21.9%	73 29.6%	96 32.1%
11-15	73 17.7%	27 8.8%	61 24.5%	61 20.3%
16-20	78 18.9%	90 29.3%	53 21.2%	73 24.5%
21-30	116 28.1%	102 33.2%	53 21.5%	30 10.1%
31 or more	52 12.6%	21 6.9%	8 3.3%	39 13.1%
Total	415 100.0%	308 100.0%	248 100.0%	300 100.0%

Note: For country-of-origin data, see Table 3.49.

TABLE 8.18 Age at Immigration, by State

Age at Immigration	*California*	*Florida*	*New York*	*Texas*
6 or younger	45 10.7%	31 9.2%	12 4.2%	27 8.0%
7-18	128 30.1%	56 16.9%	76 27.1%	135 39.9%
19-30	187 44.1%	96 29.0%	117 42.0%	117 34.6%
31 or older	64 15.0%	149 44.9%	74 26.6%	59 17.5%
Total	423 100.0%	332 100.0%	279 100.0%	339 100.0%

Note: For country-of-origin data, see Table 3.50.

TABLE 8.19 Year Received Permanent Resident (Legal Immigrant) Visa, by State

Year Received Permanent Resident Visa	*California*	*Florida*	*New York*	*Texas*
1965 or before	123 29.6%	80 25.7%	38 13.8%	72 22.1%
1966-1978	182 44.0%	151 48.4%	151 55.3%	131 40.0%
1979-1988	109 26.4%	81 25.9%	85 31.0%	124 38.0%
Total	414 100.0%	311 100.0%	274 100.0%	328 100.0%

Note: For country-of-origin data, see Table 3.53.

TABLE 8.20 Number of Visits to Home Country Per Year, by State

Visits to Home Country Per Year of Residence	*California*	*Florida*	*New York*	*Texas*
No visits	86 20.7%	220 68.3%	89 35.0%	140 43.7%
One visit per year or less	271 64.9%	97 30.0%	156 61.0%	94 29.3%
More than one and less than three visits per year	34 8.1%	4 1.1%	9 3.6%	28 8.8%
Three or more visits per year	26 6.3%	2 0.6%	1 0.4%	58 18.2%
Total	418 100.0%	322 100.0%	255 100.0%	320 100.0%

Note: For country-of-origin data, see Table 3.59.

TABLE 8.21 Close Relatives Living in Home Country, by State

Close Relatives Living in Home Country	*California*	*Florida*	*New York*	*Texas*
Yes	400 92.5%	297 88.7%	258 91.9%	310 91.2%
No	32 7.5%	38 11.3%	23 8.1%	30 8.8%
Total	432 100.0%	335 100.0%	281 100.0%	340 100.0%

Note: For country-of-origin data, see Table 3.64.

TABLE 8.22 Close Relatives Living in the United States, but Outside Household, by State

Close Relatives Living in the United States, but Outside Household	*California*	*Florida*	*New York*	*Texas*
Yes	384 89.2%	306 91.2%	238 84.8%	268 78.7%
No	47 10.8%	30 8.8%	43 15.2%	73 21.3%
Total	430 100.0%	335 100.0%	281 100.0%	340 100.0%

Note: For country-of-origin data, see Table 3.65.

Organizational Behavior, Perceptions of Discrimination, and Political Activities

Findings

Latino immigrants in Texas were the most likely to be members of community organizations (Table 8.23). In each of the states with large Latino immigrant populations, churches were the most common organizations of choice. More than two-thirds of Texas respondents and half of California Latino immigrants were church members.

Among those Texas Latinos who were organizational members, most belonged to majority-Latino organizations (Table 8.24). In California, Florida, and New York, on the other hand, Latino immigrants who were organizational members belonged to both majority Latino and majority non-Latino organizations.

The majority of California and New York Latino immigrants believed that U.S. society discriminates against Latinos (Table 8.25). Contrary to the perception that stereotyping is common in the Southwest, Texas Latino immigrants did not report the highest rates of perceived discrimination.

Regardless of state, however, more than three-quarters of Latino immigrants reported that their families had *not* experienced discrimination (Table 8.26). Among those whose families had experienced discrimination, the majority of Floridians and Texans reported that they had experienced this discrimination "rarely" (Table 8.27).

Florida Latino immigrants were the least likely and California and New York immigrants the most likely to report that the Immigration and Naturalization Service discriminates against Latinos more than other immigrant ethnic groups (Table 8.28).

Latino immigrants in New York who had immigrated as adults were the most likely to report that they had marched or followed political news in the country of origin (Table 8.29).

Types of U.S. political activity varied by state (Table 8.30). The majority of Latino immigrants in all states but California followed U.S. politics in the news. Though few overall participated in these activities, New York Latino immigrants were the most likely to have written letters about political issues; Texas Latino immigrants were the most likely to have distributed leaflets about U.S. political issues; and Florida Latino immigrants were the most likely to have contributed money or attended fundraisers. Across the seven political activities identified, California Latino immigrants were the least likely or tied for the least likely in five categories.

Questions Asked: 46, 47, 48, 48a, 54, 55, 56, 64, and 100.
Tables with Comparable Data in Latino Voices: *Latino Voices* does not report data by state of residence.

TABLE 8.23 Membership in Community Organizations, by State

Type of Organization	*California*	*Florida*	*New York*	*Texas*
Church	219 50.6% (n=432)	193 57.7% (n=335)	174 61.9% (n=281)	234 68.7% (n=340)
PTA	108 24.9% (n=432)	82 24.4% (n=335)	61 21.7% (n=281)	82 24.0% (n=340)
Sports club	68 15.7% (n=432)	51 15.1% (n=335)	38 13.4% (n=281)	43 12.7% (n=340)
Social club	53 12.4% (n=432)	43 13.0% (n=335)	41 14.5% (n=281)	11 3.2% (n=340)
National-origin club	43 10.0% (n=432)	33 9.8% (n=335)	34 12.2% (n=281)	19 5.7% (n=340)
Union	62 14.3% (n=432)	25 7.5% (n=335)	15 5.3% (n=281)	17 4.9% (n=336)
Political club	17 3.8% (n=432)	4 1.3% (n=335)	6 2.0% (n=281)	17 5.0% (n=340)
Fraternal club	8 1.8% (n=432)	36 10.7% (n=335)	12 4.2% (n=281)	3 0.9% (n=340)
Senior citizens club	13 3.0% (n=432)	9 2.6% (n=335)	9 3.1% (n=281)	4 1.2% (n=340)

Note: For country-of-origin data, see Table 4.8.

TABLE 8.24 Latinos in Organizations to Which Respondent Belonged, by State

Type of Organization	*California*	*Florida*	*New York*	*Texas*
Majority Latino church	167 76.8% (n=217)	168 87.9% (n=191)	122 70.2% (n=174)	202 86.8% (n=232)
Majority Latino PTA	48 45.8% (n=106)	38 46.6% (n=81)	16 26.3% (n=61)	63 77.1% (n=82)
Majority Latino sports club	38 56.7% (n=67)	23 45.3% (n=50)	13 35.5% (n=38)	36 83.7% (n=43)
Majority Latino social club	37 71.1% (n=52)	30 69.7% (n=43)	19 46.2% (n=41)	10 93.9% (n=11)
Majority Latino nationality club	40 92.5% (n=43)	32 98.8% (n=33)	34 100.0% (n=34)	19 100.0% (n=19)
Majority Latino union	26 45.3% (n=58)	10 39.7% (n=25)	5 34.6% (n=15)	9 54.0% (n=16)
Majority Latino political club	10 67.0% (n=16)	3 63.6% (n=4)	1 19.8% (n=6)	17 100.0% (n=17)
Majority Latino fraternal club	5 76.2% (n=6)	20 57.9% (n=35)	5 42.9% (n=12)	3 88.2% (n=3)
Majority Latino seniors club	4 27.5% (n=13)	7 85.0% (n=8)	5 53.8% (n=9)	2 61.9% (n=4)

Note: For country-of-origin data, see Table 4.9.

TABLE 8.25 Perception of Discrimination Against Latinos, by State

Does U.S. Society Discriminate Against Latinos?	*California*	*Florida*	*New York*	*Texas*
Yes	231 56.9%	139 44.0%	156 58.8%	153 48.2%
No	151 37.1%	168 53.2%	102 38.5%	160 50.2%
Unsure	24 6.0%	9 2.8%	7 2.7%	5 1.6%
Total	407 100.0%	315 100.0%	266 100.0%	318 100.0%

Note: For country-of-origin data, see Table 5.1.

TABLE 8.26 Personal or Familial Experience of Discrimination, by State

Has Respondent's Family Experienced Discrimination?	*California*	*Florida*	*New York*	*Texas*
Yes	104 24.5%	56 16.9%	42 15.2%	66 19.3%
No	321 75.5%	279 83.1%	236 84.8%	274 80.7%
Total	425 100.0%	335 100.0%	278 100.0%	339 100.0%

Note: For country-of-origin data, see Table 5.2.

TABLE 8.27 Frequency of Familial Discrimination, by State

Frequency of Familial Discrimination	*California*	*Florida*	*New York*	*Texas*
Rarely	42 40.5%	29 53.5%	17 47.2%	39 58.7%
Occasionally	37 36.2%	10 18.5%	17 46.8%	19 29.1%
Frequently	24 23.3%	15 28.0%	2 6.1%	8 12.2%
Total	103 100.0%	54 100.0%	36 100.0%	66 100.0%

Note: For country-of-origin data, see Table 5.3.

TABLE 8.28 Perception of INS Discrimination Against Latinos, by State

Does INS Discriminate Against Latinos More Than Other Immigrant Ethnic Groups?	*California*	*Florida*	*New York*	*Texas*
Yes	127 30.2%	51 15.4%	86 31.3%	78 23.2%
No	182 43.4%	181 54.5%	113 41.0%	181 53.6%
Unsure	111 26.5%	100 30.1%	76 27.7%	79 23.2%
Total	420 100.0%	333 100.0%	275 100.0%	338 100.0%

Note: For country-of-origin data, see Table 5.4.

TABLE 8.29 Participation in Home-Country Political Activity, Among Respondents Who Migrated as Adults, by State

Type of Home-Country Political Activity	*California*	*Florida*	*New York*	*Texas*
Followed political news	65 23.9% (n=271)	107 43.2% (n=249)	105 48.8% (n=215)	55 28.5% (n=192)
Marched	100 36.9% (n=270)	89 36.1% (n=247)	133 61.9% (n=215)	76 39.5% (n=192)
Voted	13 5.0% (n=270)	26 10.3% (n=250)	10 4.7% (n=213)	23 12.1% (n=192)

Note: For country-of-origin data, see Table 5.9.

TABLE 8.30 Participation in U.S. Political Activity, by State

Type of U.S. Political Activity	*California*	*Florida*	*New York*	*Texas*
Followed political news	206 47.8% (n=431)	209 62.5% (n=335)	172 61.5% (n=279)	195 58.6% (n=332)
Wrote letters about U.S. political issues	28 6.5% (n=428)	28 8.4% (n=335)	27 9.5% (n=279)	22 6.5% (n=336)
Distributed leaflets about political issues	18 4.3% (n=426)	15 4.4% (n=334)	12 4.4% (n=279)	28 8.2% (n=336)
Marched	20 4.6% (n=427)	45 13.4% (n=335)	12 4.5% (n=279)	24 7.2% (n=332)
Contributed money or attended fundraisers	78 19.7% (n=396)	129 39.4% (n=329)	80 29.0% (n=276)	61 19.1% (n=321)
Voted	23 5.7% (n=413)	31 9.3% (n=335)	38 13.6% (n=281)	32 9.5% (n=340)
Helped people register to vote	11 2.6% (n=422)	9 2.6% (n=335)	13 4.5% (n=281)	20 6.0% (n=336)

Note: For country-of-origin data, see Table 5.10.

Attachment to the United States and Attitudes Toward and Experiences with Naturalization

Findings

Virtually all Latino immigrants, regardless of state, planned to make the United States their permanent home (Table 8.31). The lowest rate by state was New York where a still high 94 percent planned to reside permanently in the United States.

Overwhelmingly, Latino immigrants reported that life was better in the United States than in the country of origin (Table 8.32). Latino immigrants in Texas were the most likely to hold this belief and Latino immigrants in Florida the least likely.

The majority of California, Florida, and Texas Latino immigrants and a near majority of New York Latino immigrants reported a national self-identification with their countries of origin (Table 8.33).

Overwhelming majorities anticipated that their children's lifestyle would be better than their own (Table 8.34). This perception was particularly strong among New York respondents.

Between 59 and 77 percent of Latino immigrants reported that becoming a U.S. citizen was "very" important (Table 8.35). Latino immigrants in Florida were the most likely to report that citizenship was "very" important and Latino immigrants in California the least likely.

More than four-fifths of Latino immigrants reported that their peers favored their becoming U.S. citizens (Table 8.36). Rates of support equaled or exceeded 95 percent in Florida and New York.

Regardless of state, the reason for naturalizing that was most likely to be ranked as "very important" was that it allowed the immigrant to vote (Table 8.37).

When asked to identify the single most important reason for naturalizing, Latino immigrants in each of the states identified the ability to participate more fully in American life (Table 8.38). More than one-third of Texas respondents identified this as the most important reason for naturalizing.

Among non-citizens in each of the states, the perception that there were no benefits in naturalizing was the reason most likely to be ranked as "very important" as a reason for not naturalizing (Table 8.39). The perception that the citizenship exam was difficult was almost as likely to be ranked as very important by Latino immigrants in California, Florida, and Texas.

Non-citizen respondents identified simply not considering naturalization as the most important reason for not naturalizing (Table 8.40).

Between 14 and 18 percent of Latino immigrants in these four states had taken English classes specifically to prepare for naturalization (Table 8.41). There was little variation by state.

A majority of Latino immigrants in California and Florida had studied U.S. history and civics (Table 8.42).

Among those who had taken U.S. history and civics, the majority in California, Florida, and New York did not take these classes to prepare for the naturalization exam (Table 8.43). The majority in Texas did take these classes to prepare for the exam.

Among those who had applied for naturalization, the majority in all states but Florida began the process in the 1980s (Table 8.44). In Florida, equal numbers began the process in 1970s as in the 1980s.

Latino immigrants in Florida who had taken the naturalization exam were the most likely to report that it was "very hard" (Table 8.45). Regardless of state, however, the modal assessment of the test was "very easy."

Questions Asked: 10, 42, 52, 53, 64, 64a, 65, 68, 70, 84c, 91, 92a, 97, 98, and 102.
Tables with Comparable Data in Latino Voices: *Latino Voices* does not report data by state of residence.

TABLE 8.31 Plans to Make a Permanent Home of the United States, by State

Plans to Make a Permanent Home of the United States	*California*	*Florida*	*New York*	*Texas*
Yes	408	327	261	338
	97.1%	99.4%	94.0%	99.4%
No	12	2	17	2
	2.9%	0.6%	6.0%	0.6%
Total	420	329	278	340
	100.0%	100.0%	100.0%	100.0%

Note: For country-of-origin data, see Table 6.1.

TABLE 8.32 Evaluation of Where Life is Better, by State

Where Life is Better	*California*	*Florida*	*New York*	*Texas*
In the United States	333 79.3%	217 67.2%	222 79.8%	297 89.6%
In country of origin	33 8.0%	81 25.0%	20 7.2%	11 3.3%
In another place	53 12.7%	25 7.8%	36 12.9%	23 7.0%
Total	420 100.0%	322 100.0%	278 100.0%	332 100.0%

Note: For country-of-origin data, see Table 6.2.

TABLE 8.33 National Self-Identification, by State

National Self-Identification	*California*	*Florida*	*New York*	*Texas*
With the United States	168 41.2%	107 32.7%	118 42.5%	122 36.9%
With the country of origin	209 51.2%	192 58.5%	138 49.6%	190 57.3%
With some other country	31 7.6%	29 8.8%	22 7.9%	19 5.8%
Total	408 100.0%	328 100.0%	279 100.0%	331 100.0%

Note: For country-of-origin data, see Table 6.3.

TABLE 8.34 Anticipations for Children's Lifestyle, by State

Expected Lifestyle of Children	*California*	*Florida*	*New York*	*Texas*
Better than respondent	293 90.8%	216 88.9%	190 97.0%	200 89.6%
Same as respondent	19 6.0%	13 5.2%	6 3.0%	22 10.0%
Worse than respondent	10 3.2%	14 5.9%	0 0.0%	1 0.4%
Total	323 100.0%	244 100.0%	195 100.0%	223 100.0%

Note: For country-of-origin data, see Table 6.4.

TABLE 8.35 Importance of Becoming a U.S. Citizen, by State

Importance of Becoming a U.S. Citizen	*California*	*Florida*	*New York*	*Texas*
Very	250 59.3%	259 77.2%	183 66.8%	209 62.6%
Somewhat	118 28.0%	57 17.0%	48 17.7%	71 21.3%
Not very	35 8.2%	9 2.6%	30 11.1%	39 11.7%
Not at all	19 4.5%	11 3.2%	12 4.5%	15 4.4%
Total	422 100.0%	335 100.0%	274 100.0%	334 100.0%

Note: For country-of-origin data, see Table 6.5.

TABLE 8.36 Peers' Attitudes Toward Respondent Naturalizing, Among Those Non-citizens Who Had Discussed Naturalization, by State

Peers' Attitudes Toward Respondent Naturalizing	*California*	*Florida*	*New York*	*Texas*
Favor	104 86.6%	103 96.3%	70 95.0%	112 80.8%
Oppose	6 4.7%	0 0.0%	4 5.0%	21 14.8%
Mixed views	10 8.6%	4 3.7%	0 0.0%	6 4.3%
Total	120 100.0%	107 100.0%	73 100.0%	139 100.0%

Note: For country-of-origin data, see Table 6.7.

TABLE 8.37 Reasons for Seeking U.S. Citizenship, by State

Reason (Ranked as Very Important)	*California*	*Florida*	*New York*	*Texas*
Naturalization allows the vote	360 83.5% (n=431)	315 94.2% (n=335)	246 88.4% (n=278)	276 86.4% (n=319)
Naturalization increases opportunities for children	332 77.9% (n=426)	255 77.2% (n=330)	237 86.2% (n=275)	261 79.8% (n=327)
Naturalization helps relatives immigrate	314 74.4% (n=422)	272 82.1% (n=332)	227 81.5% (n=278)	254 76.1% (n=334)
Naturalization offers additional legal protections	311 73.5% (n=423)	251 76.4% (n=328)	228 82.5% (n=276)	252 76.5% (n=329)
Naturalization gives children citizenship	313 73.8% (n=424)	252 76.8% (n=328)	201 73.0% (n=276)	250 74.4% (n=336)
Naturalization expands job opportunities	332 77.7% (n=427)	202 60.5% (n=334)	200 71.7% (n=279)	236 70.5% (n=334)
Naturalization establishes eligibility for government programs	282 65.9% (n=427)	242 72.8% (n=333)	191 68.9% (n=277)	243 74.0% (n=328)
Naturalization allows equal participation in American life	280 65.5% (n=427)	238 71.6% (n=333)	208 75.3% (n=277)	227 69.5% (n=326)
Naturalization improves life in general	283 66.1% (n=429)	216 64.9% (n=333)	183 66.5% (n=275)	234 70.3% (n=332)
Naturalization increases opportunities to earn money	252 60.1% (n=420)	160 49.0% (n=326)	168 60.2% (n=278)	183 54.5% (n=336)

Note: For country-of-origin data, see Table 6.11.

TABLE 8.38 Most Important Reason for Naturalizing, by State

Most Important Reason for Naturalizing	*California*	*Florida*	*New York*	*Texas*
To participate more fully in American life	99 23.0%	86 25.7%	85 30.3%	119 35.1%
To participate in American politics	84 19.3%	76 22.7%	19 6.9%	45 13.2%
To express gratitude to the United States	19 4.4%	75 22.4%	26 9.3%	14 4.1%
To attain eligibility for specific benefits	70 16.2%	18 5.2%	39 13.8%	34 9.9%
To achieve economic opportunities	68 15.8%	12 3.6%	17 6.1%	10 3.0%
To help children	11 2.5%	2 0.5%	5 1.8%	8 2.3%
To assure a better life	26 6.0%	10 3.0%	35 12.5%	26 7.7%
To resolve own or family's immigration problems	12 2.8%	10 3.1%	12 4.4%	19 5.6%
To reduce discrimination	0 0.1%	3 1.0%	2 0.6%	2 0.6%
There is no reason to naturalize	22 5.0%	22 6.7%	4 1.6%	6 1.7%
No opinion	21 5.0%	21 6.2%	36 12.9%	57 16.8%
Total	432 100.0%	335 100.0%	281 100.0%	340 100.0%

Note: For country-of-origin data, see Table 6.12.

TABLE 8.39 Reasons for Not Seeking U.S. Citizenship Among Those Who Have Not Naturalized, by State

Reason (Ranked as Very Important)	*California*	*Florida*	*New York*	*Texas*
Perception that there are no benefits in naturalization	67 23.4% (n=286)	59 35.4% (n=167)	73 39.3% (n=185)	73 28.4% (n=255)
Difficulty of U.S. citizenship exam	64 22.2% (n=288)	55 33.0% (n=167)	33 17.2% (n=192)	62 23.6% (n=263)
Latinos face discrimination in the United States	59 20.2% (n=293)	14 8.5% (n=169)	37 19.3% (n=190)	56 22.6% (n=249)
Desire to keep land in home country	51 17.6% (n=290)	10 5.6% (n=170)	32 16.9% (n=191)	61 23.4% (n=260)
Feelings of disloyalty to home country	42 14.4% (n=293)	26 15.4% (n=170)	31 16.1% (n=193)	30 12.2% (n=249)
Maintenance of political ties with country of origin	29 9.9% (n=292)	10 5.9% (n=169)	23 11.8% (n=194)	61 23.4% (n=262)
Fear of loss of culture	38 12.9% (n=295)	20 11.5% (n=170)	20 10.6% (n=192)	34 12.8% (n=265)
Fear of INS mistreatment	29 10.4% (n=281)	6 3.8% (n=169)	23 12.7% (n=183)	13 5.0% (n=263)
Plan to live permanently in home country	21 7.1% (n=292)	9 5.4% (n=171)	29 15.2% (n=194)	7 2.9% (n=252)

Note: For country-of-origin data, see Table 6.14.

TABLE 8.40 Most Important Reason for Not Seeking Naturalization, Among Non-U.S.-Citizens, by State

Most Important Reason for Not Naturalizing	*California*	*Florida*	*New York*	*Texas*
Has not considered	127 46.7%	43 33.5%	64 40.7%	79 33.6%
Love of home country	45 16.6%	18 13.8%	16 10.4%	34 14.4%
No reason to naturalize	31 11.4%	17 13.3%	18 11.3%	31 13.1%
Does not speak English	18 6.7%	17 13.2%	22 13.7%	30 12.7%
Intends to return to country of origin	23 8.6%	7 5.6%	25 15.9%	4 1.5%
Believes that it is not possible to naturalize	14 5.3%	12 9.1%	5 3.0%	26 11.1%
Desires to maintain property in home country	8 3.1%	9 7.1%	5 3.2%	21 9.0%
Other	4 1.6%	6 4.4%	3 1.8%	11 4.6%
Total	271 100.0%	127 100.0%	157 100.0%	236 100.0%

Note: For country-of-origin data, see Table 6.15.

TABLE 8.41 Study of English to Prepare for Naturalization, by State

English Study to Prepare for Naturalization	*California*	*Florida*	*New York*	*Texas*
Has not taken English classes	108 25.1%	108 32.2%	112 39.8%	151 44.5%
Has taken English classes, but not to prepare for citizenship	261 60.5%	170 50.8%	125 44.6%	129 37.9%
Has taken English classes to prepare for U.S. citizenship	62 14.4%	57 17.0%	44 15.6%	60 17.6%
Total	432 100.0%	335 100.0%	281 100.0%	340 100.0%

Note: For country-of-origin data, see Table 6.16.

TABLE 8.42 Study of U.S. History and Civics, by State

U.S. History and Civics Study	*California*	*Florida*	*New York*	*Texas*
Yes	240 55.8%	187 55.7%	96 34.1%	149 43.8%
No	190 44.2%	148 44.3%	185 65.9%	191 56.2%
Total	430 100.0%	335 100.0%	281 100.0%	340 100.0%

Note: For country-of-origin data, see Table 6.17.

TABLE 8.43 Study of U.S. History and Civics to Prepare for Naturalization, by State

U.S. History and Civics to Prepare for Naturalization	*California*	*Florida*	*New York*	*Texas*
Yes	101 23.4%	74 22.0%	34 12.1%	84 24.8%
No	138 32.0%	113 33.7%	62 21.9%	65 19.1%
Has not taken history or civics classes	193 44.6%	148 44.3%	185 65.9%	191 56.2%
Total	432 100.0%	335 100.0%	281 100.0%	340 100.0%

Note: For country-of-origin data, see Table 6.18.

TABLE 8.44 Decade in Which Applicants Began Application Process, by State

Decade in Which Respondent Obtained the Application	*California*	*Florida*	*New York*	*Texas*
1960s or before	22 13.2%	16 8.8%	24 18.0%	15 12.8%
1970s	31 18.6%	85 45.5%	23 17.2%	18 14.8%
1980s	113 68.3%	85 45.6%	85 64.8%	86 72.4%
Total	166 100.0%	186 100.0%	132 100.0%	119 100.0%

Note: For country-of-origin data, see Table 6.26.

TABLE 8.45 Difficulty of the Citizenship Exam, by State

Difficulty of the Citizenship Exam	*California*	*Florida*	*New York*	*Texas*
Very hard	5 5.1%	18 14.9%	5 6.8%	3 7.7%
Somewhat hard	18 18.1%	17 14.1%	13 19.3%	5 11.6%
Somewhat easy	30 30.0%	28 23.4%	23 34.0%	16 34.7%
Very easy	46 46.8%	57 47.5%	27 39.8%	21 46.0%
Total	99 100.0%	119 100.0%	67 100.0%	45 100.0%

Note: For country-of-origin data, see Table 6.38.

Appendix 1: Survey Questionnaire

Hello, I'm .... We are conducting a survey about the citizenship process in this country and the experiences of people who have immigrated here from other countries. Our aim is to gather information that will help us assist individuals who are interested in becoming U.S. citizens. The survey is sponsored by the National Association of Latino Elected and Appointed Officials (NALEO). (NAME OF LOCAL LATINO OFFICIAL) is a member of this organization. Everything that I ask you will be kept completely confidential. Your name will not be connected in any way with the findings of this study. In order to determine whom I am to interview, I need to ask some questions about your household.

Household Eligibility Screener

A. First, are there any adults in this household of Hispanic or Latino origin or descent? By Hispanic or Latino origin, we mean people who can trace their ancestry to a Spanish-speaking country.
B. Were any of the Hispanic or Latino heritage adults in this household born *outside* the United States or Puerto Rico?
C. Did any of these foreign-born adults of Hispanic or Latino heritage legally immigrate to the United States *before* 1983?
D. Are any of these foreign-born adults legal immigrants who have been married for three years or more to someone who has been a U.S. citizen for three years or more?
E. How many persons 18 years of age or older live in this household?
F. Starting from the oldest (male/female) in this household, tell me the first name or initial of each adult (male/female) in this household and continue with the next oldest (male/female) and so on until we have listed all the (men/women).
G. Now I would like to know the age of each adult in this household. Starting with (FIRST PERSON ON ROSTER). How old was (he/she) on (his/her) last birthday?
H. (LIST GENDER FOR EACH ADULT IN HOUSEHOLD).
I. What is (PERSON's) relationship to you?

J. In what country was (PERSON) born?
K. In what year did (PERSON) immigrate to the United States?
L. Is (PERSON) a United States citizen?
M. Does (PERSON) have papers as a permanent resident alien?
N. Now I would like to ask about those people 17 years of age or younger who live in the household. How many children 17 or younger live here? Like before, I would like to make a list of all members of your household 17 or younger. Just give me the first name or initial of each one.
O. How old was (CHILD) on (his/her) last birthday?
P. What is (CHILD's) relationship to you?
Q. Was (CHILD) born in the United States or in some other country?

Naturalization Survey

I would like to start the interview by asking you some questions about your life here in the United States and in your own country to help us create a picture of the immigration process. This information is completely confidential and you will never be identified personally.
1. Of what country were you a citizen when you immigrated to the United States?
2. Was the area you lived in before coming to the U.S.:
   A rural, or less populated area, or
   An urban, or city area?
3. How old were you when you came to the U.S. to live permanently?
4. When you first came to the U.S. to live permanently, did any of your family members come with you at that time? What about friends and associates? Did any friends come with you?
   Family members only.
   Friends only.
   Both family and friends.
   Came alone.
5. Thinking about when you first came to the U.S. to live permanently, were any of your family members *already* living in this country?
   Family members only.
   Friends only.
   Both family and friends.
   Knew no one in the United States.
5a. Were any of these (family members, friends, associates) U.S. citizens at that time?
6. In what year did you get your permanent resident visa?
7. When you first got your permanent visa, did you plan to make the United States your permanent home?
8. When you first got your resident visa, what was your *most* important reason for coming to the U.S. to live?

To join family members,
To flee political strife,
To flee communism,
To avoid deportation due to illegal status,
For specific job/employment,
Economic reasons/make money,
Immigrated with parents,
Immigrated with spouse, or
Other. (specify)

9. Did you originally obtain a resident visa, green card, or *mica* because you were:

A refugee,
The parent of a U.S. citizen,
The child of a U.S. citizen,
The brother/sister of a U.S. citizen,
The spouse of a U.S. citizen,
The child of a permanent resident alien,
The child of parents who legally immigrated,
Qualified as a professional,
Qualified as a result of your job, or
Something else? (Specify)

10. Do you presently plan to make the United States your permanent home?
11. Why do you think people might return to their home country to live?

To retire.
After saving enough money.
When the political situation changes at home.
When children have grown up.
To get married.
Other. (Specify)

12. Counting both long and short stays, how many times have you returned to your home country since you obtained your permanent visa?
13. Counting all stays, what was the total number of years you lived in the U.S. before you became a permanent resident?
14. Do you still have close relatives living in your home country?
15. How long have you lived in this area?
16. Now I have some questions about your family. *Not counting* the people living in this household, do you have any other relatives living in the United States?
17. Are any of these relatives U.S. citizens?
18. Has your father or your mother become a U.S. citizen, or do they not live in the U.S?
19. The next questions are about the kinds of work that you and your family have done. Did you ever work for pay in your home country?
20. Have you ever worked for pay in the United States?

21. Since you came here to live permanently, have you had any periods of unemployment that have lasted six months or longer when you were looking for a job, but could not find one?

22. Think about the first job you took after coming to the United States to live permanently. What kind of work did you do? What were your duties? What kind of business was this in?

23. Was this job:
Full-time, or
Part-time?

24. And currently, which of the following best describes your present employment situation? Are you:
Working full-time,
Working part-time,
Temporarily laid off,
Jobless and looking for work,
A student,
A homemaker,
Retired,
Disabled, or
Something else? (Specify)

25. What kind of work do you (did you) usually do? What are (were) your duties? What kind of business is (was) this in?

26. How long have you worked (did you work) for this employer?

27. Are you (Were you) working at more than one job?

28. Are (Were) *most* of your coworkers:
Latinos,
Non-Hispanic whites,
Blacks,
Asians,
Something else? (Specify)
Works alone or in family business.

29. For this job is (was) a speaking knowledge of English:
Very important,
Somewhat important,
Not very important, or
Not important at all?

30. How satisfied are (were) you with this job? Would you say:
Very satisfied,
Somewhat satisfied,
Not very satisfied, or
Not satisfied at all?

31. Does anyone in your family:
Own your home,

Rent for cash, or
Do you have some other arrangement?

32. In what year did you purchase your home?
33. Now I would like to ask you some questions about your education. How many years of school have you completed and received credit for?
34. What is the highest degree or diploma, if any, that you hold?

34a. Was that degree earned in the U.S. or in another country?

35. What is your current marital status? Are you:
Married,
Separated,
Divorced,
Widowed, or
Have you never been married?
36. Has your husband/wife ever worked for pay in the U.S.?
37. Is your husband/wife presently:
Working full-time,
Working part-time, or
Not in labor force?
38. What kind of work does (did) he/she usually do? What are (were) his/her duties? What kind of business is (was) this in?
39. What is the highest grade of schooling your husband/wife completed and received credit for?
40. What was the highest degree or diploma he/she received?

40a. Was this in the United States or another country?

41. Do you presently have any children living in the U.S.?
42. Thinking about your lifestyle now, including your job, your home, and your leisure activities, do you think that when your children are your age, their lifestyle in this country will be:
Better than yours is now,
About the same as yours is now, or
Not as good as yours is now?
Don't know.
43. Now I'd like to ask you some questions about your friends and neighbors in the U.S. Are *most* of the people in your neighborhood:
Latinos,
Non-Hispanic whites,
Blacks,
Asians, or
Something else? (Specify)
44. Would you say that of your close friends in the U.S.:
All are Latino,
Most are Latino,
Some are Latino, or
None are Latino?

45. Would you say that of most of your Latino friends in the U.S.:
  Most are U.S. citizens,
  Some are U.S. citizens,
  Few are U.S. citizens, or
  None are U.S. citizens?
46. In your home country, did you ever participate in politics in any of the following ways:
  Following politics in the news?
  Canvassing/marching?
  Voting in elections?
  Never participated in politics?
47. In the United States, have you ever participated in politics in any of the following ways:
  Following politics in the news?
  Writing letters?
  Distributing literature?
  Canvassing/marching?
  Attending fundraisers/contributing money?
  Voting in elections?
  Helping people register and vote?
  Never participated in politics?
48. Since you have lived here in the United States, have you been a member of, or participated in, any of the following types of organizations?
  A church?
  A labor union?
  A Parent Teachers type Association (PTA)?
  A sports club?
  A senior citizens club?
  A fraternal order such as the Masons or Lions?
  A political club or group?
  A club whose members are people from your home country?
  A social club?
  Some other type of club?
48a. Are the majority of the members of that organization Latino?
49. Are you currently registered to vote in the United States?
50. Did you vote in the:
  1984 Presidential election?
  Last state election?
  Last county or municipal election?
  Last school board election?
51. Do you identify yourself as a:
  Republican,
  Democrat,
  An independent,

Some other party, or
Are you unaffiliated?

52. Thinking about your life in general, which has been better:
Life here in the United States, or
Life in the home country?
Other. (Specify)

53. Which of the following best describes how you see yourself:
More as an American,
More as a member of your home country, or
As something else? (Specify)

54. Do you think that North Americans discriminate against Latinos?

55. Have you or has any member of your family experienced any discrimination or hostility from North Americans?

56. Has this happened:
Hardly ever,
Occasionally, or
Frequently?

57. Some people follow politics while others do not. Can you tell me the names of the following politicians:
The vice president of the United States?
The governor of your state?

58. The next questions are about the languages you use. What language do you *usually* speak at home?
English,
Spanish, or
Both English and Spanish?

59. When you read newspapers, are the papers that you *usually* read written in:
Spanish, or
English?
Both equally.
Never read the newspaper.

60. When you listen to the radio, are the stations that you *usually* listen to broadcast in:
Spanish, or
English?
Both equally.
Never listen to the radio.

61. When you watch television, do you *usually* watch:
Spanish, or
English?
Both equally.
Never watch TV.

62a. Would you say that you understand spoken English:
Very well,
Well,
Not very well, or
Not at all?

62b. Would you say that you speak English:
Very well,
Well,
Not very well, or
Not at all?

62c. Would you say that you write in English:
Very well,
Well,
Not very well, or
Not at all?

62d. Would you say that you read in English:
Very well,
Well,
Not very well, or
Not at all?

63. Now I am going to read you a few statements in English and I would like you to translate them into Spanish. It is not necessary that you understand all of each statement; just translate as much as you can.
He raises his hand.
It is very cold.

64. The next set of questions concerns activities related to the citizenship process. Since coming to the United States to live permanently have you ever studied:
The English language?
The history and government of the United States?

64a. Did you do this to help you become a U.S. citizen?
The English language?
The history and government of the United States?

65. In your opinion, what is the most important reason for becoming a citizen of the United States?

66. At the time you became a U.S. citizen were you:
Never married,
Married,
Widowed,
Divorced, or
Separated?

67. Have you or has someone helping you ever tried to get an application form for U.S. citizenship from the Immigration and Naturalization Service, that is, the INS?

68. Did you actually get the application form?
69. Why haven't you been able to get an application form?
70. In what year did you first try to get the application for U.S. citizenship?
71. Did any person or organization help you get the application form, or did you get it by yourself?
72. From whom did you get this help?
73. Did you pay any money to get this help?
74. How much did you pay for this help?
75. Have you ever filed an application for U.S. citizenship with the INS?
76. Do you plan to file an application in the future?
77. Why have you not filed an application for citizenship?
78. How many times in all have you filed an application for U.S. citizenship with the INS?
79. Has the INS ever asked you to resubmit the citizenship application?
80. Why were you asked to resubmit your application?
81. Did you refile the application form?
82. Have you ever taken the citizenship exam?
83. The following questions are about the exam for U.S. citizenship. How many times have you taken the citizenship exam?
84. Let's talk about the (first) exam for citizenship that you took.
84a. In what year did you take it?
84b. In what city did you take it?
84c. Overall was the exam:
 Very hard,
 Somewhat hard,
 Somewhat easy, or
 Very easy?
84d. What parts of the exam did you find the hardest?
84e. Was the INS examiner:
 Helpful,
 Rude, or
 Neither one?
84f. Was the exam given in:
 English,
 Spanish, or
 Both English and Spanish?
84g. How many questions were asked?
84h. Did you feel that the questions were fair?
84i. Did you pass the exam?
84j. What, if anything, will/did you do to better prepare yourself for the next exam?
85. Do you plan to take the citizenship exam (again)?
86. Have you already scheduled (rescheduled) the exam?
87. Is the exam scheduled in the future?

88. Have you ever missed taking the citizenship exam when you had an appointment to take it?
89. Why did you miss the exam?
90. Will you reschedule the exam?
91. For you, is (was) becoming a U.S. citizen:
   Very important,
   Somewhat important,
   Not very important, or
   Not important at all?
92. Have you ever seriously discussed the possibility of becoming a U.S. citizen with
   Members of your family?
   Your friends?
   Your employer?
   Your clergyman?
   Anyone else?
92a. Did they favor or oppose your becoming a U.S. citizen?
93. At the present time, do you have any definite plans to apply for U.S. citizenship?
94. How much money, in total, do you think it costs to become a U.S. citizen? Would you say:
   Less than $100,
   $100 to $200,
   $201 to $500,
   $501 to $1,000, or
   More than $1,000?
   Didn't know it cost.
   Don't know.
95. U.S. citizenship can be denied for several reasons. If you were to apply for, or have applied for citizenship, do you have any reason to believe you might be denied for *any* reason?
96. Why do you think you might be denied citizenship?
   Criminal conviction.
   Receive welfare/public assistance.
   Engage in illegal activity.
   Other. (Specify)
97. What is the *most important* reason you decided to remain a citizen of your home country.
98. I'm going to read you some reasons for *not* becoming a U.S. citizen. For each one, please tell me if it is a very important, somewhat important, not very important, or not at all important reason for you not becoming a citizen:
   You plan to return to your home country someday to live there permanently.

You feel that there is discrimination against Latinos in the U.S.
You are afraid of losing the culture of your home country.
You want to maintain political ties with your home country.
You think the INS exam will be too difficult.
You would lose your property rights in your home country.
You would feel disloyal to your home country.
You feel you would be mistreated by the INS.
There are no real benefits to becoming a citizen.
Any other reason? (Specify)

99. People have different views about how the INS treats people who apply for citizenship. We are interested in your opinions about how the INS treats people. When people apply for citizenship, do you think the INS is:
Helpful, or
Unhelpful?
Neither.

100. In comparison to other immigrant ethnic groups in the U.S., do you think the INS discriminates against Latinos?

101. Overall, how satisfied are you with the way you have been treated by the INS? Would you say:
Very satisfied,
Somewhat satisfied,
Somewhat dissatisfied, or
Very dissatisfied?
No experience with the INS.

102. Next, I will read you some statements about becoming a U.S. citizen. For each one, please tell me if it is a very important, somewhat important, not very important, or not at all important reason for becoming a U.S. citizen.
Citizenship helps you get a better job.
Citizenship helps you earn more money.
Citizenship makes you eligible for U.S. government programs.
Citizenship enables your children to become U.S. citizens.
Citizenship helps your relatives immigrate to the U.S. more quickly.
Citizenship allows you to vote in U.S. elections.
Citizenship allows you to participate more equally in American life.
Citizenship provides greater opportunities for your children's future.
Citizenship makes your life better overall.
Citizenship offers you more protection under the law.
Any other reason? (Specify)

103. Have you ever served in the United States Armed Forces?

104. Do you own a video cassette recorder (VCR)?

105. Now I would like to ask you a few final questions that are for descriptive purposes only. Considering the income of all persons in this household last month before taxes and including all sources such as wages, profits, interest,

government payments, and such, was your total monthly household income:

Less than $1,500, or
Over $1,500?

106. Which of the following categories best estimates your total household income last month?

Less than $500,
$500 to $800,
$801 to $1,200, or
$1,201 to $1,499?

107. Which of the following categories best estimates your total household income last month?

$1,500 to $2,000,
$2,001 to $2,500,
$2,501 to $3,000, or
$3,001 or more?

108. Do you currently receive income from any of the following:

Social Security?
Aid to Families with Dependent Children (AFDC)?
Food stamps?
Medicaid or Medicare?
Educational assistance programs?
Supplemental Security Income?
Veteran's benefits?
Housing subsidy?
Any other government assistance program? (Specify)

109. What is the zip code where you live?

110. We may want to contact you again someday in the future to find out more about your immigration to the United States and how life is going for you here. Would you be willing to let us interview you again someday?

111. Would you be willing to give me your name and address, in the event that we might want to contact you by mail?

112. Would you be willing to give us the name, address, and phone number of two people who would always know how to contact you in the event that you move and we are unable to locate you for another interview?

Appendix 2: National Latino Immigrant Survey Methodology

The National Latino Immigrant Survey (NLIS) was developed by the National Association of Latino Elected Officials (NALEO) Educational Fund as part of a multi-year research and demonstration project to assess the reasons for low rates of naturalization in the Latino community. The survey was designed to measure Latino immigrant attitudes about and experiences with life in the United States and, more specifically, with naturalization. The Ford Foundation funded the NLIS.

The survey was conducted under the overall direction of NALEO's National Director, Harry Pachon. At the time of the study, Dr. Pachon was Kenan Professor of Politics at Pitzer College. Eve Fielder of the Survey Research Center at the University of California, Los Angeles served as project director. From the project's inception, Louis DeSipio served as project research associate. Karen Escalante of the NALEO Educational Fund coordinated the laborious process of translating and back-translating the survey instrument to ensure that the language in the Spanish version was generic to all of Latin America and the Caribbean. The activities of each of these project staff members benefited from the insights and guidance of the project's Social Science Advisory Board: Dr. William A. Diaz of the Ford Foundation, Dr. Leo Estrada of the University of California, Los Angeles, Dr. Alejandro Portes of Johns Hopkins University, and Dr. Lou Tornatzky of the Industrial Technology Institute.

The project engaged the services of several consultants for specialized phases of the research. The Institute for Survey Research at Temple University conducted a survey pre-test. Robert Santos coordinated Temple's efforts. Dr. Martin Frankel developed the sample and the weighting for the final results. Dr. Paul Planchon of the U.S. Department of Education assisted in the development of the survey questionnaire. Elrick and Lavidge, Inc. collected survey data under the direct supervision of Ms. Fielder. Finally, Dr. Homer Garcia of Baylor University converted the raw data tape into a user-friendly data file and coordinated the coding of the open-ended questions.

Survey Pre-Test

The impetus for the study was the discovery that little scholarly analysis existed on the reasons for low rates of naturalization in the Latino community. This discovery raised a dilemma. The absence of such prior studies made us wonder whether it was possible to survey Latino immigrants about their experiences with immigration and naturalization. We identified two likely problems with carrying out such a survey. First, there was the sensitivity of the subject matter. In order to guarantee a national sample, some argued that we would have to do in-person interviews, a methodology largely precluded by the project's budget. The second potential limitation also related to budgetary questions. We were concerned that the scarcity of this population would making screening costs prohibitively high.

In order to evaluate the gravity of these possible impediments, NALEO engaged Temple Survey Research to conduct a pre-test of the National Latino Immigrant Survey. Temple documented that Latino immigrants were willing to answer questions about their experiences with immigration and naturalization as well as about life and work experiences in the United States. They also documented that the targeted population—Latino immigrants with five or more years of permanent residence (three if married to a U.S. citizen who had been a citizen for three or more years)—though rare, could be reached through a telephone survey. They also developed a concrete measure of the time needed to administer the survey instrument to naturalized citizens and to naturalization-eligible non-U.S.-citizens.

The National Latino Immigrant Survey

Sample

The data for the National Latino Immigrant Survey were derived from telephone interviews conducted between August and November 1988 with a two-stage, stratified probability sample, developed by Dr. Martin Frankel, of foreign-born Latino immigrants living in the United States. In order to balance the goal of this study—to reach a nationally representative sample—with available resources and due to the relatively low density of foreign-born Latino immigrants legally residing in the United States (less than 2 percent of the total 1980 U.S. population), the study population was restricted to forty-seven counties. These forty-seven counties accounted for 80 percent of all foreign-born Latinos living in the United States at that time. By restricting the study population to these forty-seven counties, the incidence rate was raised to 6.8 percent (lowering the required household screening rate from approximately one in fifty-five to one in fifteen). The forty-seven counties in the sampling frame were in eight states:

Arizona, California, Florida, Illinois, Maryland, New Jersey, New York, and Texas.

The first stage of sampling involved selecting a probability sample of telephone numbers within each of the forty-seven study counties. Within each county, all telephone numbers were given an equal probability of selection. In the first stage of sample selection, each county made up a separate population stratum. Thus, the design involved forty-seven strata in total. The allocation of the first stage sample size among the various strata was proportional to a linear combination of the estimated proportion of Latino foreign–born population and the square root of this proportion. Each of these components was given equal weight, representing a compromise between statistical optimization and base-count optimization.

The second stage of sample selection was selecting respondents. We chose respondents randomly from among the qualifying persons in the household. If a household had two or more qualifying individuals, the probability of selection for the respondent was 1/M, where M is the number of eligibles in the household. The range of eligible adults in a given household was from one to eight, with 2.18 being the mean number of eligibles per household.

Respondent

To be eligible for this study, respondents needed to be all of the following:

- of Latino origin;
- born in a Spanish-speaking country other than Puerto Rico or Spain;
- a legal immigrant to the United States before 1983 or married for three years or more to someone who had been a U.S. citizen for three or more years; and
- 18 years of age or older.

Because the goal of this study was to examine the naturalization process, Puerto Ricans were excluded from the sample. Further, because the overwhelming majority of Latino immigrants to the United States are from Mexico, the Caribbean, and Central and South America, individuals born in Spain were excluded from the sample in an attempt to maintain a degree of cultural homogeneity. Additionally, we excluded immigrants born in Brazil and other non-Spanish-speaking Latin American and Caribbean countries.

We called a total of 74,430 telephone numbers. Of these, 26,212 were non-residential or non–working numbers and 8,475 were not successfully contacted after six attempts. Of the 39,743 determined residences, 25,876 had no Latinos in the household, 8,944 either refused the screening or terminated during screening, and 4,923 households had a Latino resident. Among

Latino households, 2,942 had no household members who met the screening criteria. Of the remaining 1,985 qualified households, we interviewed 1,636.

We can compute a variety of non–response rates for the sample. We did not contact 11.6 percent of the telephone numbers. Of identified households, 22.5 percent either refused or terminated during the screening. Of households screened and qualified, 17.6 percent refused.

Survey Procedures and Measures

The fieldwork for this study was conducted by Elrick and Lavidge, Inc., a commercial survey research organization headquartered in San Francisco, with branch offices throughout the United States. Elrick and Lavidge collected these data using a Computer-Assisted Telephone Interviewing (CATI) system. The large scope of this effort required that data collection be divided between two field offices—San Francisco and Atlanta. The San Francisco field operation worked with the California/Arizona sample while Atlanta covered the remaining six states. The proportional distribution of the sample was about equally divided due to the overwhelming proportion of sampled telephone numbers in California. A total of twenty-eight Spanish-speaking professional interviewers worked on the survey—thirteen in Atlanta and fifteen in San Francisco. Of the twenty-eight interviewers, twenty-four were foreign-born. The average length of interview was approximately thirty-five minutes. Interviews were conducted in either English or Spanish, with 87.4 percent electing to be interviewed in Spanish. Interviewing was conducted seven days a week, from 3:00 p.m. to 9:00 p.m. weekdays and from 9:00 a.m. to 9:00 p.m. on weekends. All non-contacted telephone numbers were attempted at least six times on varying days of the week and times of day.

The interviews inquired about a wide range of immigration-related issues. The survey questions were adapted from previous immigration and naturalization surveys and from items developed by the survey's Social Science Advisory Committee, and by experts in the fields of immigration, naturalization, and Latino political research.

We ascertained study eligibility and citizenship status by asking about ethnic origin, country of birth, year of immigration to the United States, and residency/citizenship status. Respondents who answered that they were naturalized citizens were asked a series of questions specifically about their experiences with the naturalization process and INS, while permanent resident aliens were asked a series of questions designed to assess their desire to naturalize and their actions to achieve this end. We asked all respondents about life in their country of origin, the immigration process, and about life in the United States.

The data presented here have been weighted to compensate for differential probabilities of selection, to further compensate for certain impacts of differential non–response, and to diminish the impact of certain random sampling variation. We calculated two sample weights for this study. The first weight (PWEIGHT) projects each case to its full proportion equivalent to the sum of which is approximately 1,559,296. The second weight, used in this analysis, RWEIGHT, is equal to the full population weight (PWEIGHT) divided by a constant chosen so that the sum of RWEIGHT is equal to the true sample size of 1,636. We derived PWEIGHT by multiplying the number of persons eligible for interview within the household by the product of the then-current estimate of the total number of households in the county over the number of cooperating households that produced a completed interview, times the sample estimated household eligibility rate.

About the Book

Including a foreword by Rodolfo O. de la Garza, this volume sets forth a pathbreaking social and demographic portrait of Latino legal immigrants, comparing and contrasting them with the broader Latino population and discussing for the first time, based on survey research data, the experiences of Latinos from Central and South America. Supplemented by survey questionnaires and a discussion of methodological issues, *New Americans by Choice* examines the information environment and associational and electoral behavior, their attachment to the United States, and their attitudes toward U.S. citizenship. The book follows the lead of its companion volume, *Latino Voices: Mexican, Puerto Rican, and Cuban Perspectives on American Politics.*

About the Authors

Harry Pachon is the Kenan Professor of Politics at the Claremont Colleges and President of the Tomas Rivera Center, a national institute for policy studies. He teaches at the Claremont Graduate School and Pitzer College. He is the coauthor of *Hispanics in the United States* (with Joan Moore) and the author of numerous scholarly articles. Prior to joining the Tomas Rivera Center, he served as National Director and founding board member of the National Association of Latino Elected Officials (NALEO) Educational Fund.

Louis DeSipio is a visiting assistant professor in the Department of Politics at Mount Holyoke College. He is the author and editor of a five-volume series on Latino political values, attitudes, and behaviors published by Westview Press. His study of the potential impact of the Latino vote, *Counting on the Latino Vote: Latinos as a New Electorate,* will be published in 1995 by the University Press of Virginia. He has also taught at Wellesley College.

